RSCM Anthems *for* Sopranos, Altos *and* Unison Men

30 anthems for the church year, selected and edited by David Ogden

THE ROYAL SCHOOL OF CHURCH MUSIC
19 The Close, Salisbury, Wiltshire, SP1 2EB, England
Tel: +44 (0)1722 424848
Email: press@rscm.com Website: www.rscm.org.uk
Registered charity 312828

RSCM Anthems for Sopranos, Altos and Unison Men

This book is dedicated to the memory of our friend and colleague, Gordon Appleton.

RSCM Catalogue Number: RAB83
Order Number: B0445
ISBN: 978-0-85402-280-9

Project Editor: Tim Ruffer
Cover design: Anthony Marks
Music Engraving: Donald Thomson
Printed in Great Britain by Short Run Press Ltd, Exeter.

Contents

Seasonal and Thematic Index

Introduction

This book provides a comprehensive collection of 30 anthems by 23 composers, for church and school choirs. It includes specially commissioned anthems by established composers including Philip Moore, Richard Shephard and Philip Wilby, as well as works by such newer writers as Owain Park, Ghislaine Reece-Trapp, Amy Summers and Toby Young. There are also some new arrangements of classics such as Brother James' Air and John Rutter's A Gaelic Blessing. Popular RSCM composers Thomas Hewitt Jones, Piers Maxim, Sarah MacDonald, Peter Nardone and Geoff Weaver have also contributed new works.

Many of the pieces have been tried and tested by choirs in worship. They employ a wide range of interesting and inspiring texts that echo the themes of the Sunday readings, as well as familiar words that have been given a new lease of life by inventive and imaginative settings.

No choir will feel short-changed by these three-part settings. Each composer has set about creating something original rather than reducing existing material. Many of the pieces are flexible so they can comfortably be sung by smaller groups. The organ parts are straightforward and can be also be played on the piano.

I hope you will take the time to explore the variety of anthems in this book and that they will enrich your worship. I'm sure your choir will enjoy singing them.

David Ogden
Feast of Saint Luke the Evangelist, 2018

1. All creatures of our God and King

Words: WILLIAM HENRY DRAPER (1855–1933)
based on the 'Cantico di Frate Sole' of
St. Francis of Assisi (1182–1226)

Music: ROSEMARY FIELD

9
burn - ing sun with gol - den beam, thou sil - ver moon with
f
p
12
ALTOS mf
Al - le - lu - ia,
p
p
mf
sof - ter gleam: O praise him, Al - le - lu - ia, al - le - lu - ia,
legato
+ SOPRANOS
16
f
ALTOS mf
al - le - lu - ia!
Dear
f
mf

+ SOPRANOS
19
mo - ther earth, who day by day un - fold - est bles-sings on our way, O

23
praise him, Al - le - lu - ia! The
SOPRANOS

26
flow'rs and fruits that in thee grow, let them his glo - ry al - so show! O

30
p
mp
mf
f
SOPRANO
ALTO
praise him,
Al - le - lu - ia,
al - le - lu - ia,
al - le - lu - ia!
MEN
f
mf
f
4
34
UNISON
f
Let all things their cre - a - tor bless, and
f
1
5 3 1
f
38
mf
wor - ship him in hum - ble - ness, O praise him,
Al - le - lu - ia!
mf
3

42
f
Praise, praise the Fa - ther, praise the Son, and
f
1
1
f
45
div.
praise the Spi - rit, Three in One: O praise him,
mf
SOPRANOS
48
mf
mp
ALTOS p
Al - le - lu - ia, al - le - lu - ia! al - le - lu - ia,
p
p

51
SOPRANOS & ALTOS
pp
al - le -
pp
al - le - lu - ia,
pp
pp
54
- lu - - ia!
57
legato

2. Author of life divine

Words: CHARLES WESLEY (1707–1788) *Music:* RICHARD SHEPHARD

pre - serve the life thy - self hast giv'n,
13
SOPRANO
ALTO
bread, pre - serve the life thy - self thy - self hast giv'n, and
MEN
pre - serve the life thy - self hast giv'n. and

17
mp
feed and train us up for heav'n.
feed and train us up for heav'n.
mp

22

26
mf
2. Our nee - dy souls sus - tain with fresh sup - plies of
30
mf
till all thy life we gain, and all thy full - ness
love,
34
f
prove, and, streng-thened by thy per - fect grace, be -
f

38
hold with - out a veil thy face,
42
rit. al fine
be - hold with - out a veil thy face.
pp
pp
rit. al fine
pp

Written for Christopher Connett and the choir of St Michael and All Angels, Mickleham

3. The Call

Words: GEORGE HERBERT (1593-1633)
from *'The Temple'* (1633)

Music: STUART BEER

Smooth and flowing (♩ = 92)

Sw. *mp*

ORGAN

Solo *mf*

16'+Sw. *mp*

7

mf SOPRANOS & ALTOS

Come my Way, my Truth, — my Life: Such a Way, as

Sw.

13

gives — us breath: Such a Truth, as ends all — strife: —

20

Such a Life, as kill - eth death.

Solo

26

SOPRANO
ALTO

mf

Come, my Strength:

MEN

mf

Come, my Light, my Feast, my Strength:

Sw.

31

Such as shows a feast: Such a

Such a Light, as shows a feast: Such a Feast, as

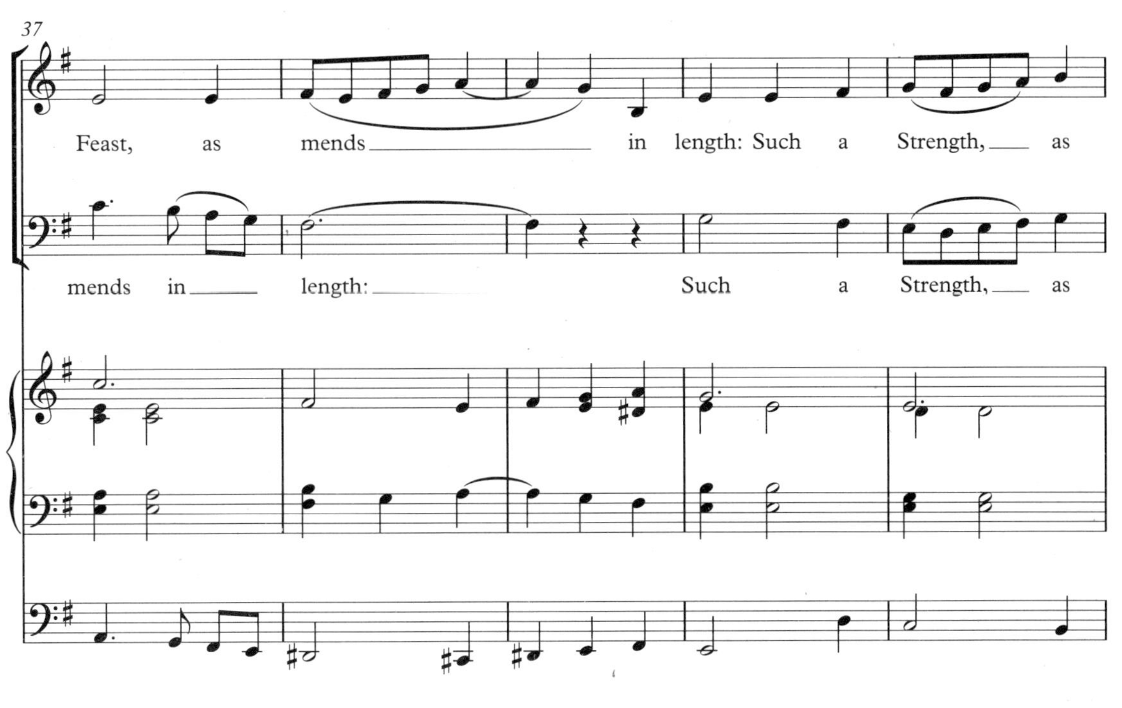
37
Feast, as mends in length: Such a Strength, as
mends in length: Such a Strength, as

42
makes his guest.
makes his guest.
Solo
poco cresc.

47

SOPRANO *f*

Come, my Joy, my Heart: Such a

f ALTO

Come, my Joy, my Love, my Heart: Such a Joy, as

f MEN

Come, my Heart: Such as

Sw.

mf

53

Joy, as none can move: Such a Love, as

none can move: Such a Love, as none can part:

none can move: Such a Love, as none

59
poco rit.
a tempo
none can part: Such a Heart, as joys in love.
Such a Heart, as joys in love.
can part: Such a Heart, as joys in love.
poco rit.
a tempo
Solo
64
rit.
rit.

4. Come, dearest Lord

Words: Isaac Watts (1674-1748)
based on Ephesians 3.16-21

Music: Philip Moore

8
div.
mf
then shall we know and taste and feel the joys, the
mf
Optional accompaniment
mf
12
joys that can - not be ex - pressed.
cresc. poco a poco
16
f
2. Come, fill our hearts with in - ward strength,
f
f

height and
19
make our en-lar-ged souls pos - sess and learn the height and
22
un poco rall.
p
breadth and length of thine im - mea-sur- a - ble grace.
p
un poco rall.
p
25
a tempo
f UNISON
3. Now to the God
f
a tempo
cresc. poco a poco
f

Rectory Cottage
30 iv 18

To Fr. André Hart on the Silver Anniversary of his Ordination, SS Peter and Paul 2017

5. Forth in the peace of Christ we go

Words: JAMES QUINN, SJ (1919-2010) *Music:* DAVID OGDEN

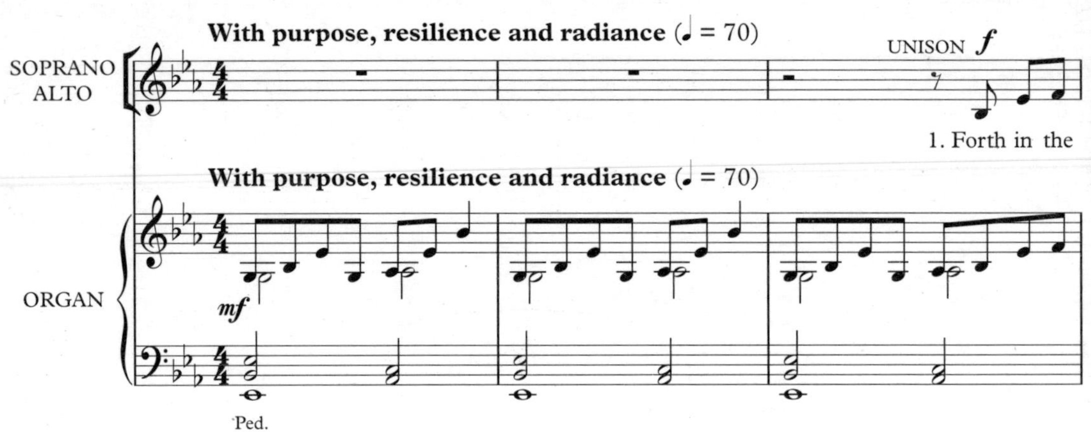

12
king.
MEN
f
2. King of our hearts, Christ reigns in
15
us; king - ship with him his ser - vants gain; with Christ, the
18
Ser - vant - Lord of all, Christ's world we serve to
21
share Christ's reign.

Poco più mosso

SOPRANOS & ALTOS

24 *mp*

3. Priests of the world, Christ sends us forth

Poco più mosso

mp

28

this world of time to con - se - crate,

MEN

32 *p*

our world of sin by grace to heal,

p

36

Christ's world in Christ to re - cre - ate.

40
mf
mp
4. Pro - phets of Christ, we hear his word:
mf
For rehearsal only
mp
pp
44
DESCANT (Small group) f
he claims our
SOPRANOS & ALTOS
he claims our minds to search his ways;
MEN
mf
48
lips, to speak his truth, his truth; he
f
he claims our lips, to speak his truth;
f

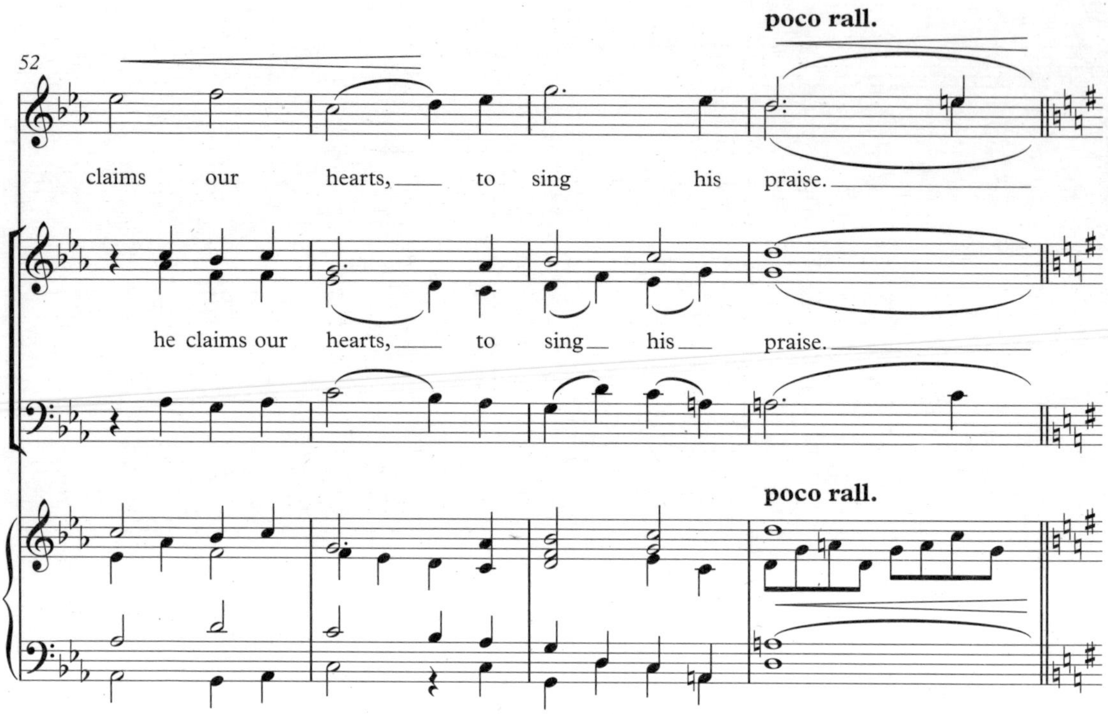
poco rall.
52
claims our hearts, to sing his praise.
he claims our hearts, to sing his praise.
poco rall.

56
UNISON
ff
Tempo I
5. We are his Church, he makes us one: here is one
ff
5. We are his Church, he makes us one: here is one
ff
Tempo I
ff

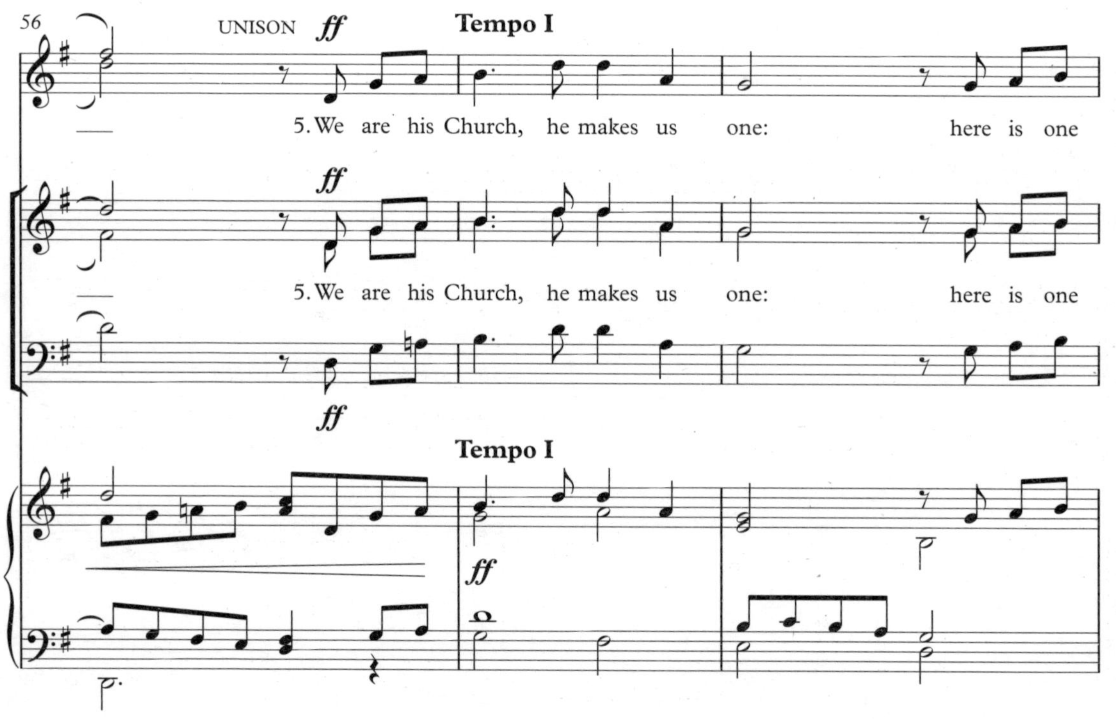

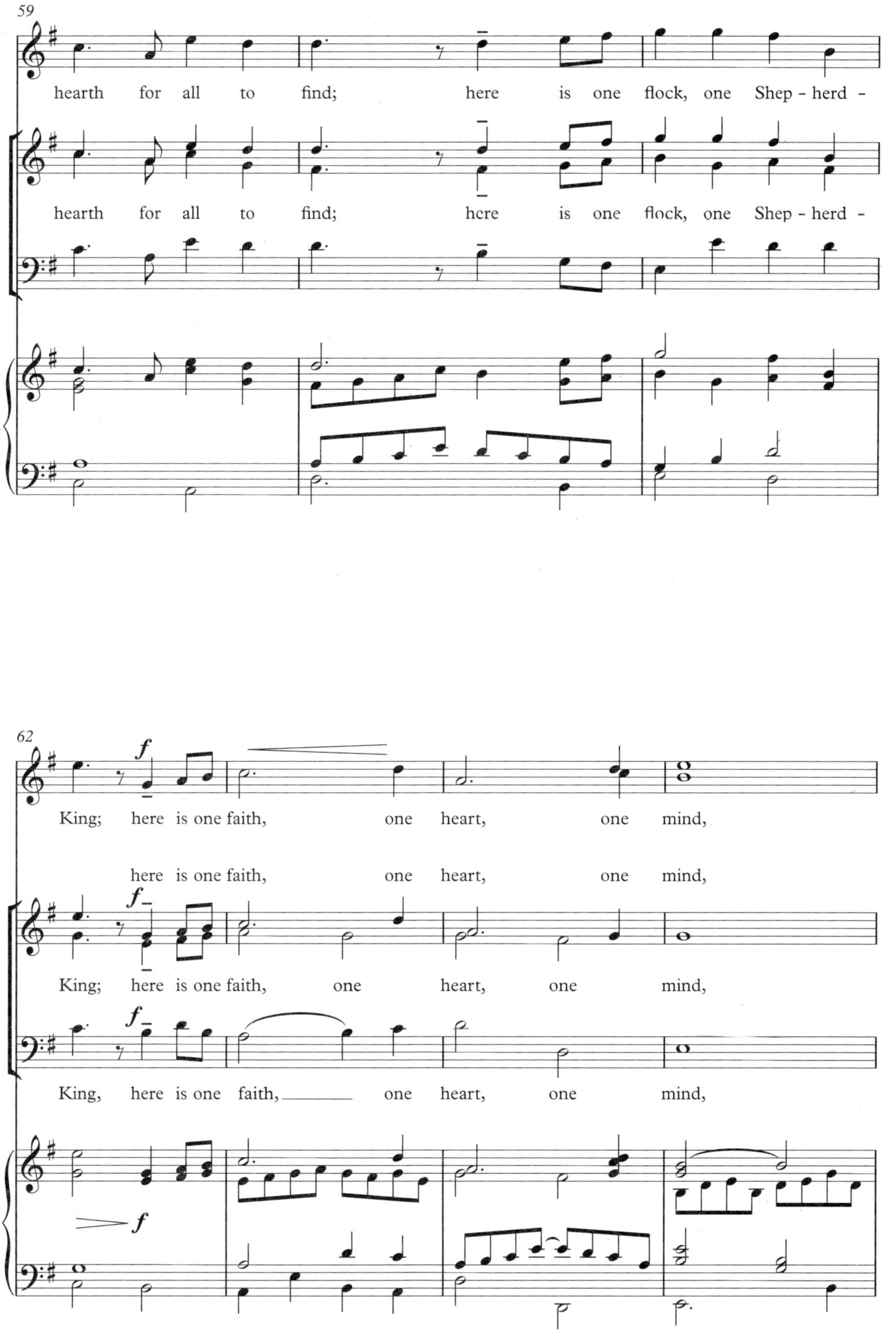

62

f

King; here is one faith, one heart, one mind,

here is one faith, one heart, one mind,

f

King; here is one faith, one heart, one mind,

f

King, here is one faith,______ one heart, one mind,

f

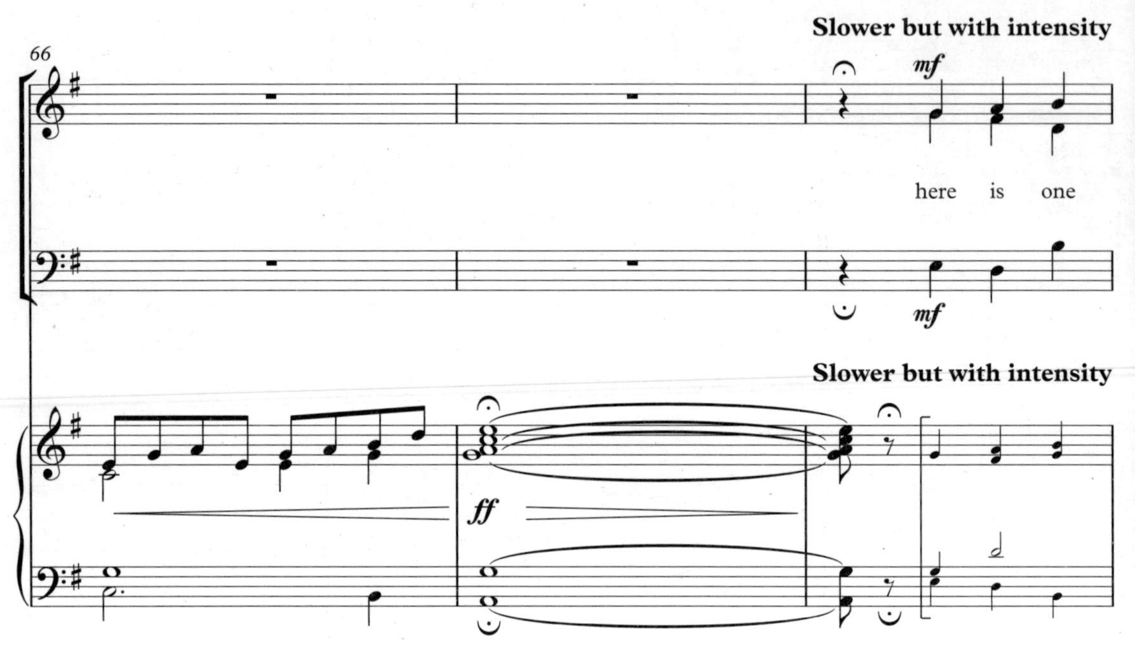
66
Slower but with intensity
mf
here is one
mf
Slower but with intensity
ff

69
mp
faith, one heart, one mind.
mp
mp
p

Commissioned by the Chancel Choir, First United Methodist Church, Omaha, USA, for Mel Olson

6. A Gaelic Blessing

Words: WILLIAM SHARP (1855–1905) *Music:* JOHN RUTTER

9
air to you, Deep peace of the qui-et
air to you, Deep peace of the
air to you, Deep peace of the

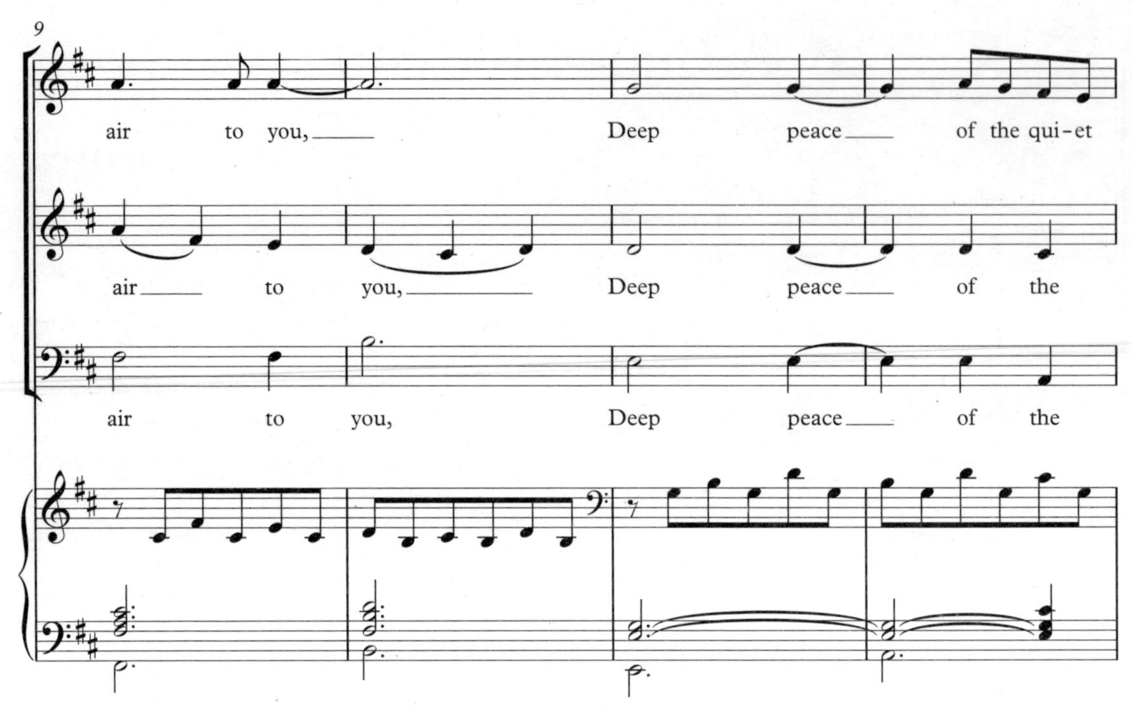

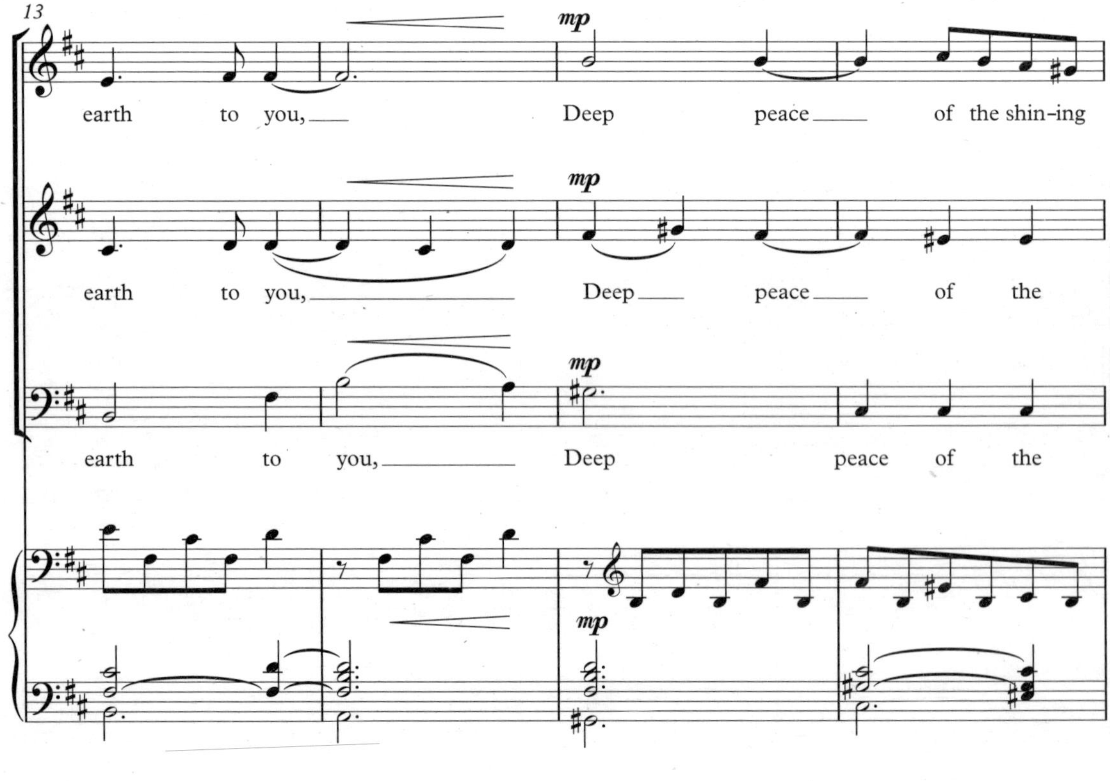

13
mp
earth to you, Deep peace of the shin-ing
earth to you, Deep peace of the
earth to you, Deep peace of the

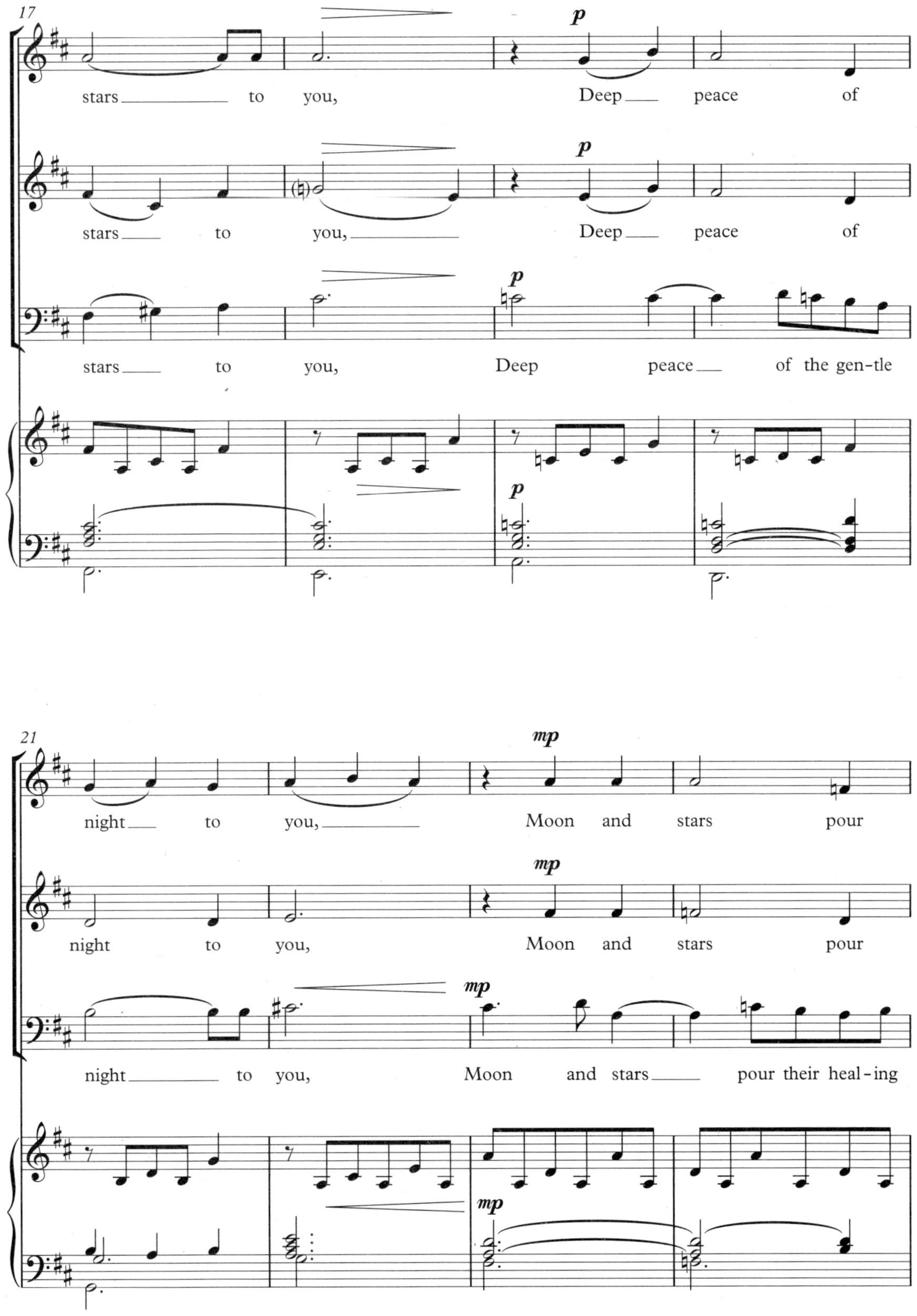

17

p

stars to you, Deep peace of

p

stars to you, Deep peace of

p

stars to you, Deep peace of the gen-tle

p

25

p

light on you, Deep peace of

p

light on you, Deep peace of

p

light on you, Deep peace of

p

29

cresc. *mf cresc.*

Christ, of Christ the

cresc. *mf cresc.*

Christ, of Christ the

cresc. *mf cresc.*

Christ, of Christ the

cresc. *mf cresc.*

33
f
dim.
light of the world to you,
f
dim.
light of the world to you,
f
dim.
light of the world to you,
f
dim.
37
mp
dim.
rall.
pp
Deep peace of Christ to you.
mp
dim.
pp
Deep peace of Christ to you.
mp
dim.
pp
Deep peace of Christ to you.
rall.
mp
p
dim.
pp

7. Hosanna to the Son of David

Words: MATTHEW 21.9 *Music:* THOMAS HEWITT JONES

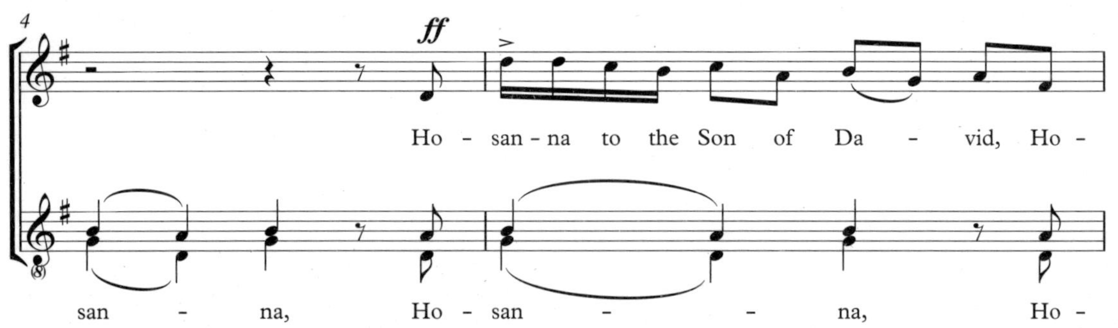

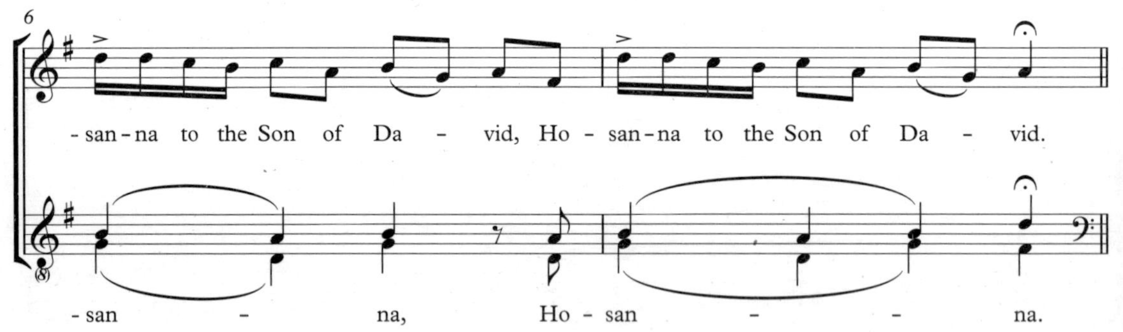

12
ff
King that com-eth in the name of the Lord. Ho - san - na, Ho -
ff
16
f
ff
- san - na, Ho - san - na, Ho - san - na. Ho -
f
21
ALL VOICES *(divide as required)*
div.
- san - na, Ho - san - na, Ho - san - na, Ho -
24
ff
Ho - san - na to the Son of Da - vid, Ho -
ff
- san - na, Ho - san - na, Ho -
26
fff
- san - na to the Son of Da - vid, Ho - san-na to the Son of Da - vid.
- san - na, Ho - san - na.
fff

for Mary

8. Holy Spirit, truth divine

Words: Samuel Longfellow (1819–1892) *Music:* Meirion Wynn Jones

Sustained and with movement (♩ = *c*.72)

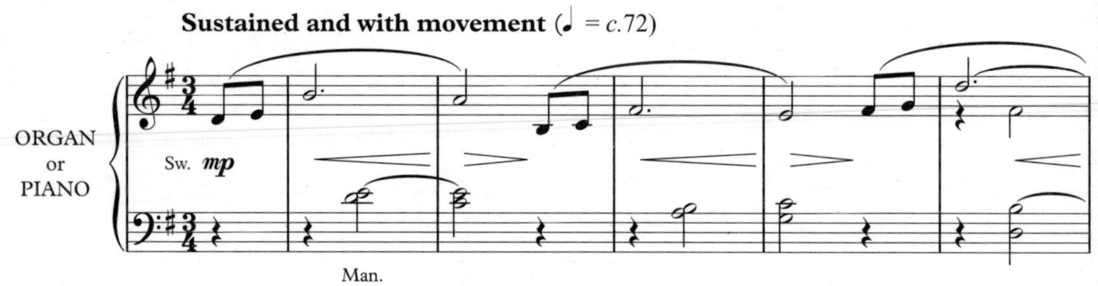

15
sight.
Gt.
Gt.
Ped.
dim.
19
SOPRANOS
mp
ALTOS
2. Ho - ly Spi - rit, love di - vine, glow with - in this heart of
MEN
mp
mp
cresc.
23
mine; kin-dle ev - 'ry high de - sire; pe-rish self in thy pure fire.

28
mf
3. Ho - ly Spi - rit, pow'r di -
mf
cresc.
mf
33
più f
-vine, fill and nerve this will of mine, by thee may I strong - ly live, brave - ly
più f
mf
38
bear and no - bly strive.
f

43
mf
cresc. poco a poco
48
SOPRANO DESCANT (optional)
mf
Ho - ly Spi - rit,
OTHER VOICES mf
4.Ho - ly Spi - rit, law di - vine, reign with
f
mf
53
law di - vine, be my law, and I shall be
più f
in this soul of mine; be my law, and I shall be firm-ly bound, for e - ver
cresc.

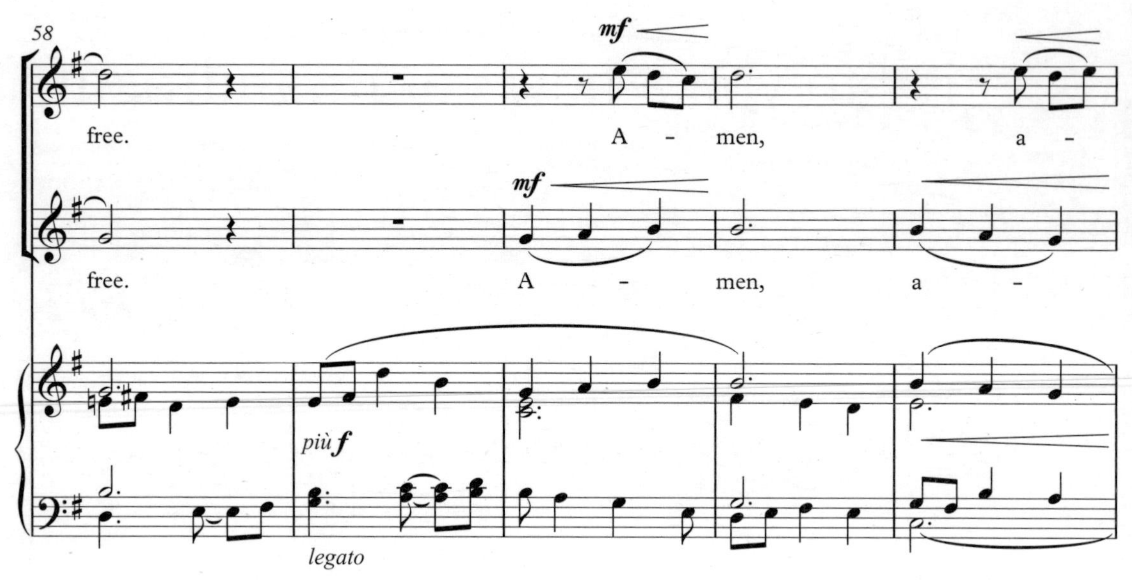
58
mf
free.
A - men, a -
mf
free.
A - men, a -
più f
legato

63
f
men, a - men.
f
men, a - - men.
molto dim.
Sw. mp
Man.

68
rall.
dim.
pp
Ped.

9. I give to you a new commandment

Words: based on JOHN 15 & 1 CORINTHIANS 13

Music: PETER NARDONE

16
unis.
p
-o - ther as I have loved you, as I have loved you. I
21
SOPRANOS & ALTOS
give to you a new com - mand - ment, a
MEN
p
U - bi ca - ri - tas est ve - ra, De - us i - bi est.
Sw. p
25
div. mf
new com - mand - ment I give to you, that you
Con - gre - ga - vit nos in u - num Chri - sti a - mor.
Gt. mf

29
UNISON
love one an - o - ther, love one an - o - ther as
Ex-sul-te - mus et in i - pso iu-cun-de-mur.
33
I have loved you, as I have loved you.
Ti-me-a - mus et a-me - mus De-um vi - vum.
37
SOPRANOS & ALTOS div.
I give to you a
I give to you a
MEN

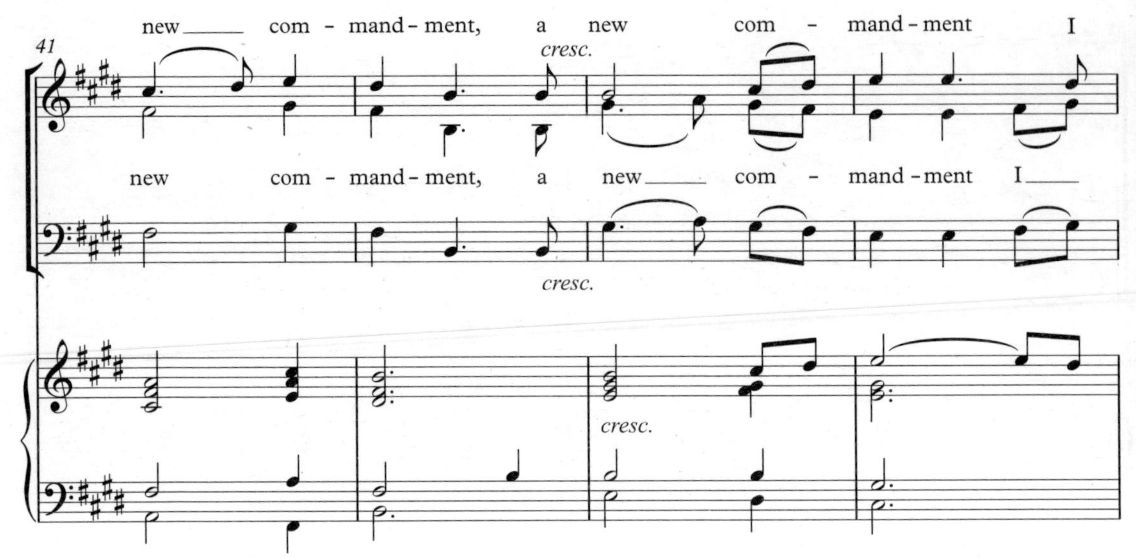

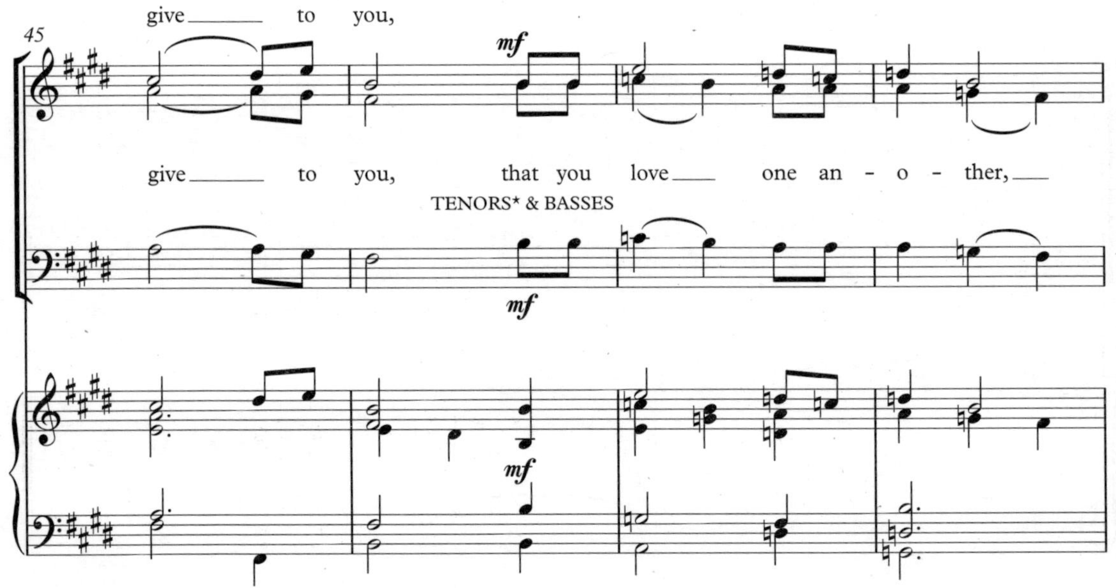

* If Tenors are available, they may sing the Soprano line down an octave from bars 45–50.

49
UNISON rit.
love one an - o - ther as I have loved you, as
Et ex cor - de di - li - ga - mus
rit.

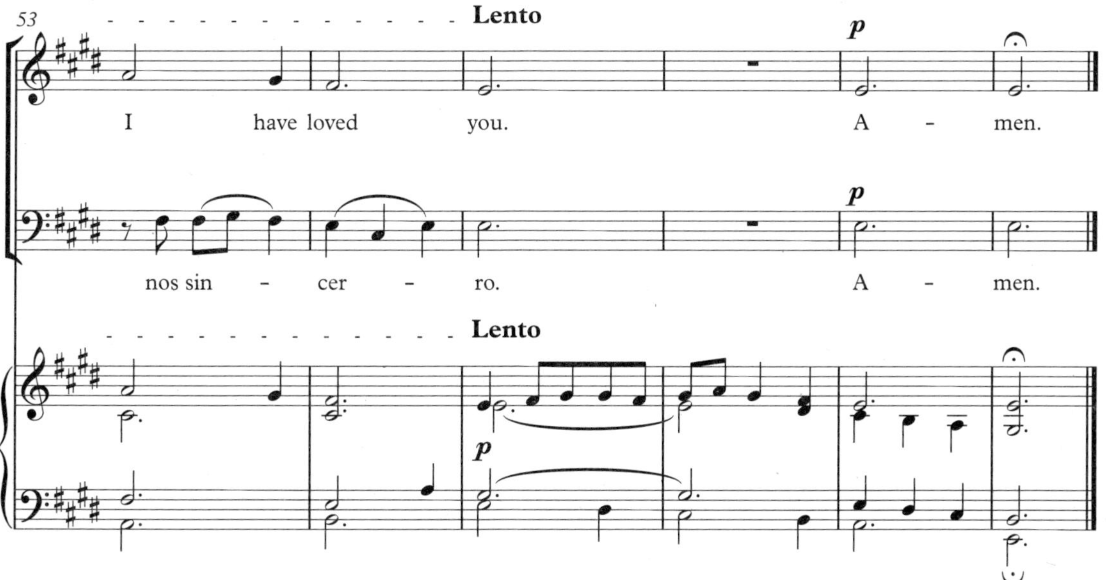
53
Lento
p
I have loved you. A - men.
p
nos sin - cer - ro. A - men.
Lento
p

In Memory of Gordon Appleton (1947–2018)

10. I will sing with the spirit

Words: Andrew Kirk
based on I Corinthians 14.15
and The Chorister's Prayer

Music: Andrew Kirk

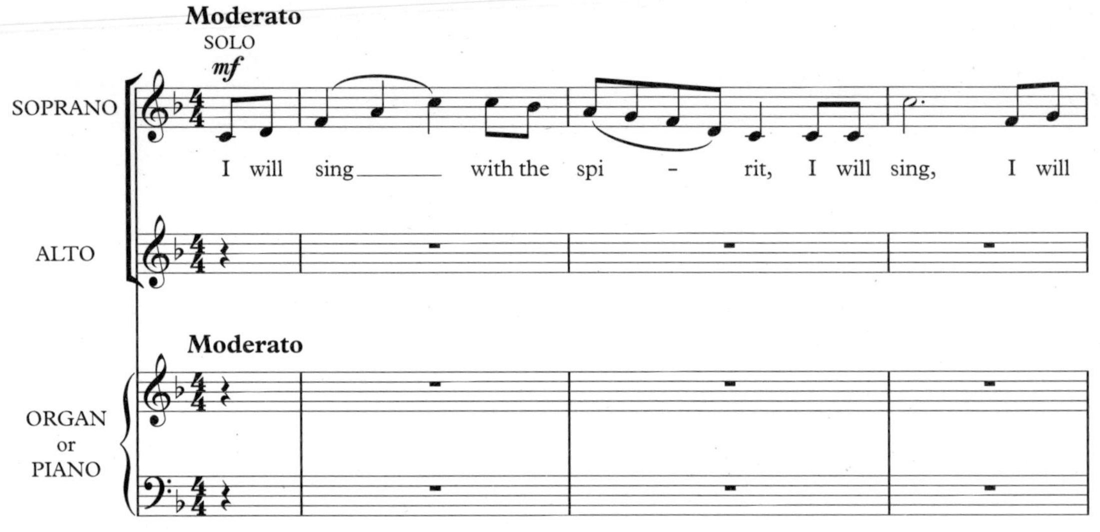

8
ALL f
— what we sing with our lips — we may be - lieve — in our hearts, I will
sing
MEN f
what we
mf

11
sing, I will sing, what we be - lieve in our hearts — we may shew
sing with our lips — we may be - lieve — in our hearts, I will sing, I will

14
(SOPRANOS)
forth_ in our lives, I will sing, I will sing, I will
(ALTOS)
what we be - lieve in our hearts_ we may shew forth_ in our lives
MEN f
sing I will

17
sing, I will sing, will sing,
and I will sing with the un - der - stand - ing
mf
sing with the un - der - stand - ing, I will

20

mf

I will sing, I will

mf

I will sing, I will sing,

sing I will sing,

26
SOPRANO SOLO mf
I will sing with the spi - rit, I will sing, I will

30
sing, ng
ALTO SOLO mf
I will sing with the spi - rit, I will sing, I will

34
ALL f
what we sing with our lips we may be - lieve in our hearts, I will
sing
MEN f
what we
mf
f

37
sing, I will sing, what we be - lieve in our hearts _ we may shew
sing with our lips _ we may be - lieve _ in our hearts, I will sing, I will

40 SOPRANOS
forth _ in our lives, I will sing, I will sing, I will
ALTOS
what we be - lieve in our hearts _ we may shew forth _ in our lives,
MEN *f*
sing,
I will

43
sing,
I will sing,
I will sing,
f
And I will
And I will
And I will

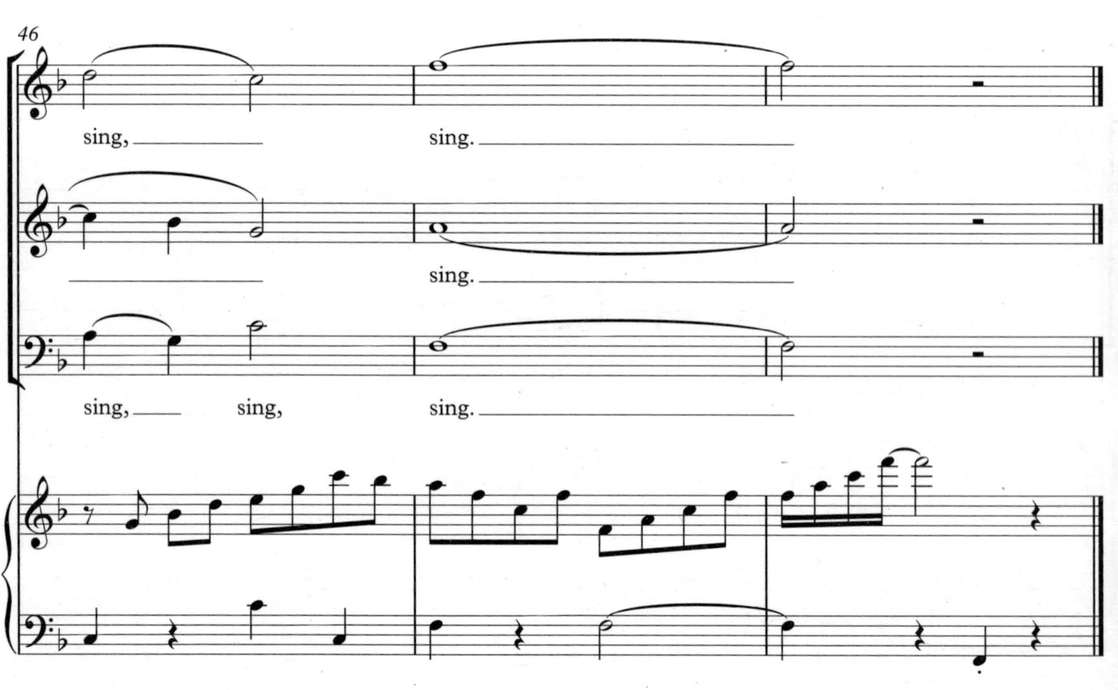
46
sing,
sing.
sing.
sing, sing,
sing.

11. An Irish Blessing

Words: Traditional Irish Blessing

Music: PHILIP WILBY

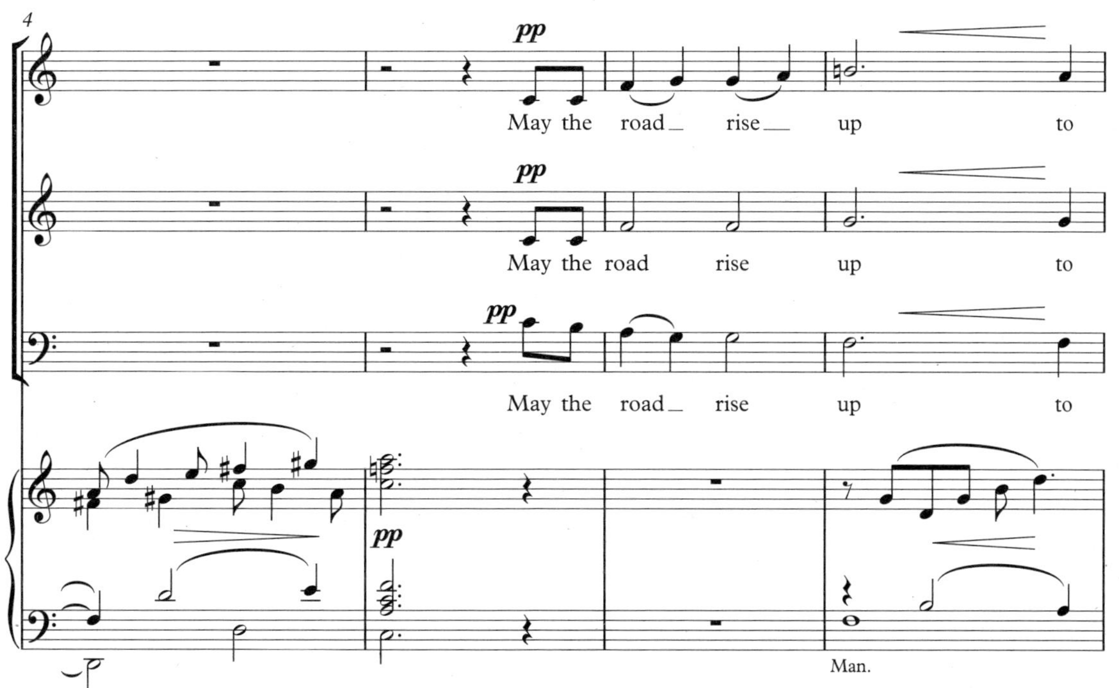

8

mp *p cresc.*

meet _ you, may the wind be al - ways at your

mp *p cresc.*

meet _ you, may the wind be al - ways at your

mp *p cresc.*

meet you, may the wind be al - ways at your

mp (Add)

Ped. Man.

Più animato

12

f

back, may the

f

back, may the

f

back, may the sun,

Più animato

f

Ped.

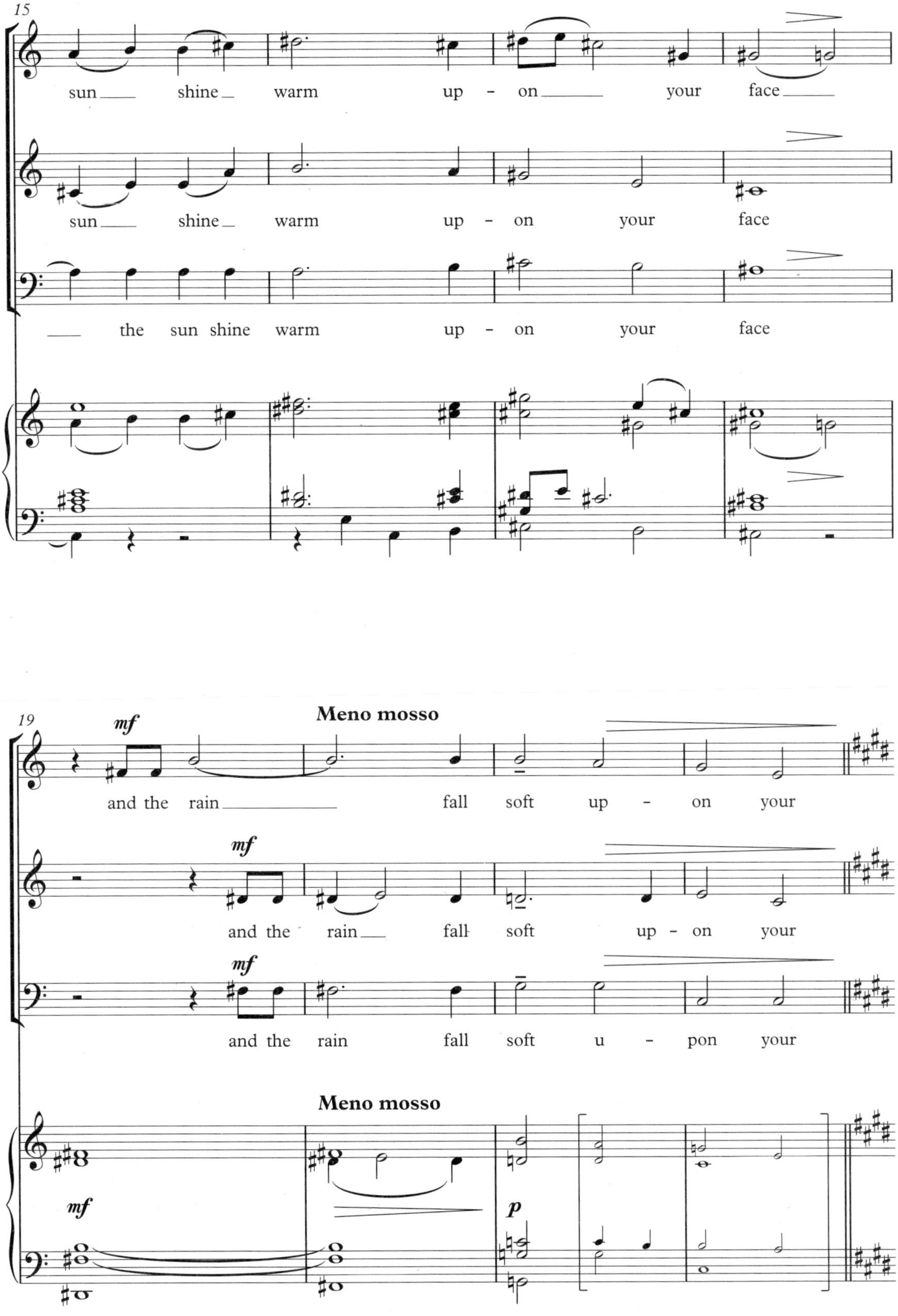

19

mf

Meno mosso

and the rain fall soft up - on your

mf

and the rain fall soft up - on your

mf

and the rain fall soft u - pon your

Meno mosso

mf

p

23

Piacevole

fields.

p *mp*

fields. And un - til we

p *mp*

fields. And un-

Piacevole

p *mp*

26

mp

And un - til we meet a -

f

meet a - gain, may God

- til we meet a - gain,

29

f *dim.*

- gain, may God hold

dim.

hold you, may God hold

f

may God hold you, may God hold

f *dim.*

33

dim. sempre *pp*

you, may God hold you,

pp

you,

dim. *pp*

you,

pp

37

Legato

pp

may God hold you in the palm of his

pp

may God hold you in the palm of his

pp

may God hold you in his

Legato

41

hand.

hand.

hand.

pp

12. Long ago on Patmos Island

Words: PAUL WIGMORE (1925–2014) *Music:* PIERS MAXIM

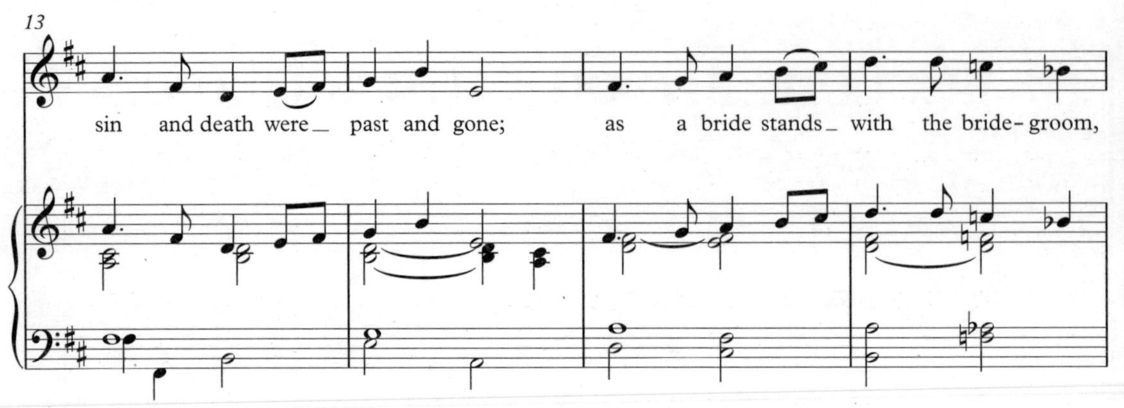
13
sin and death were past and gone; as a bride stands with the bride-groom,

17
God and all man - kind were one.
mp

21
mp SOPRANOS & ALTOS
2. In the beau - ty all a - bout us, fer - tile earth and sky and sea,
MEN
mp
Ped.

25
in the good-ness of our loved ones,_ of our friends and friends to be —
29
in these dai - ly__
in these life - time bless-ings we can see God's_ lov - ing hand,_
33
we can hear his_ call to fol - low
we___ fol - low on the road that_ he has planned.

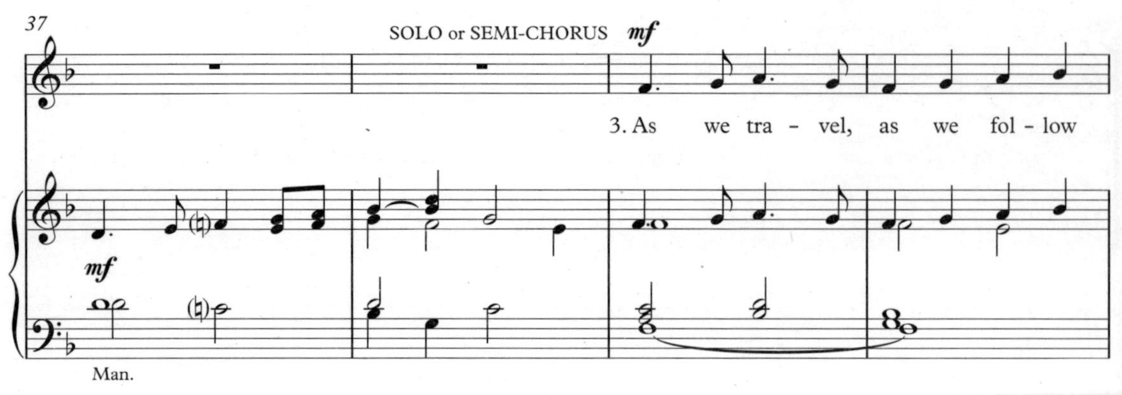
37
SOLO or SEMI-CHORUS mf
3. As we tra - vel, as we fol - low
mf
Man.

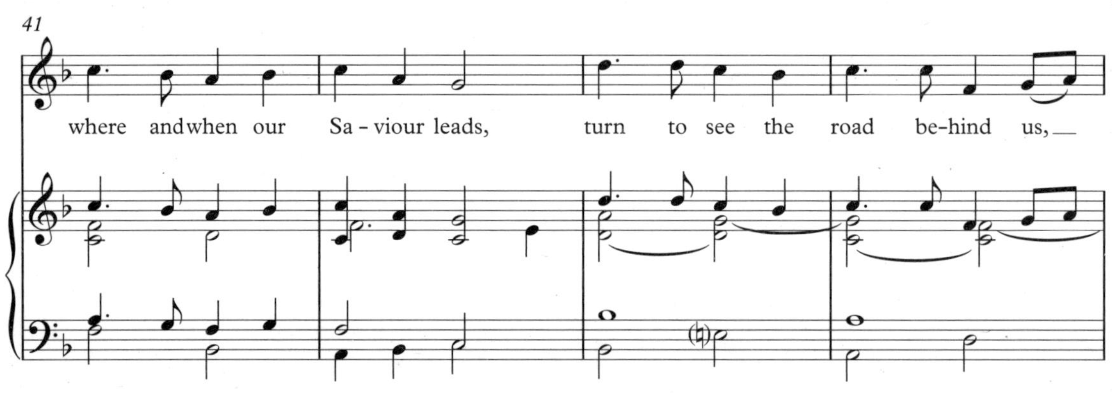
41
where and when our Sa - viour leads, turn to see the road be-hind us,

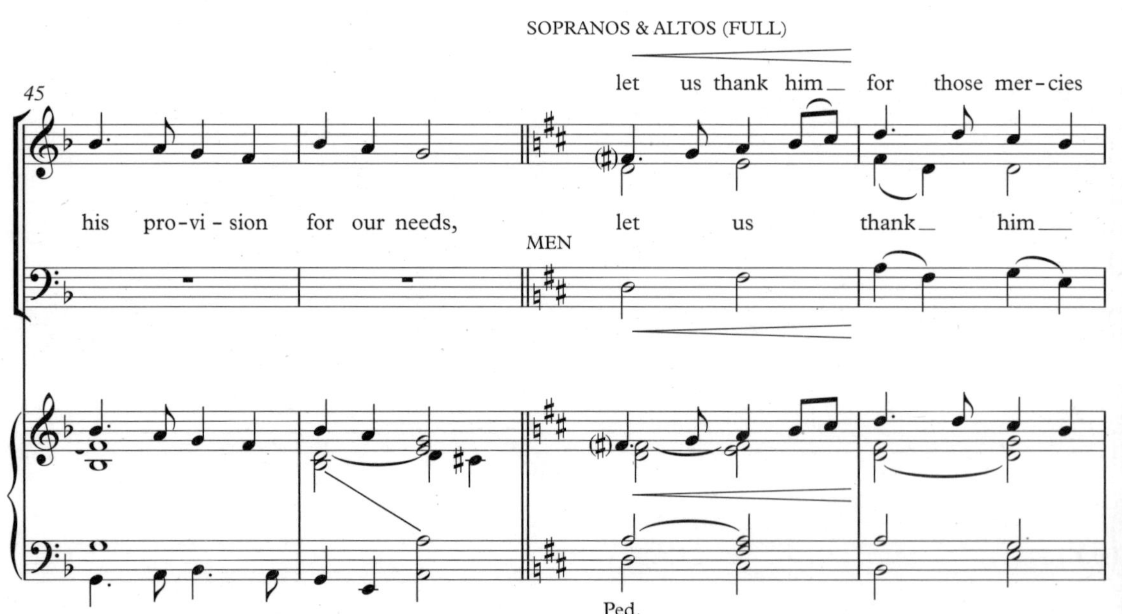
45
SOPRANOS & ALTOS (FULL)
let us thank him for those mer - cies
his pro-vi - sion for our needs, let us thank him
MEN
Ped.

49
un - de - served and free - ly giv'n,
thus on earth we find our un - ion
53
with our Lord and God in heav'n.
mf
Man.
57
poco rit.
ALL VOICES (unis.)
a tempo
f
4. May the grace of our Lord Je - sus,
f
Ped.
f dolce
61
grace that brings us in - ward peace,
with the love of God the Fa - ther

and the friend-ship of his Spi- rit —
love that makes our love in-crease, and the Spi - rit —
Senza rall.
bles - sed Ho - ly Tri - ni - ty, be with us as in that vi - sion,
Senza rall.
Meno mosso
mp
poco rit.
God with us in u - ni - ty.
mp
poco rit.
Meno mosso
mp
p
Man.

For the choir of Horfield Parish Church, Bristol

13. The Lord's my Shepherd

Words: PSALM 23
SCOTTISH PSALTER (1650)

Music: 'BROTHER JAMES'S AIR'
JAMES LEITH MACBETH BAIN (1860–1925)
arranged by GLYN JENKINS

9
p
pas-tures green; he lead-eth me the qui-et wa - ters by; he
p
p
13
lead-eth me, he lead-eth me the qui-et wa-ters by.
lead - eth, he lead - eth, the wa - ters by.
SOPRANOS & ALTOS (unis.)
mf
2. My
17
soul he doth re - store a-gain, and me to walk doth make with -
mp
Man.

21
in the paths of right-eous-ness, e'en for his own name's sake; with -
25
- in the paths of right-eous-ness, e'en for his own name's sake.
29
MEN p
3.Yea, though I walk through
p
Ped.
33
death's dark vale, yet will I fear none ill; for thou art with me,
mf
mf

37
SOPRANOS & ALTOS
p
thy rod and staff me
thy rod and
(MEN)
and thy rod and staff me com - fort still,
p
p
41
com-fort still, me com - fort still.
SOPRANOS & ALTOS (unis.)
mf
staff me com - fort still. 4. My ta - ble thou hast
mp
Man.
45
furn - ish - ed in pre - sence of my foes; my head thou dost with

49
oil a-noint, and my cup o - ver - flows; my head thou dost with

53
oil a-noint, and my cup o - ver - flows.
mf
Ped.

58
f broadly
5. Good - ness and mer - cy all my life shall__ sure-ly fol - low
f broadly
f

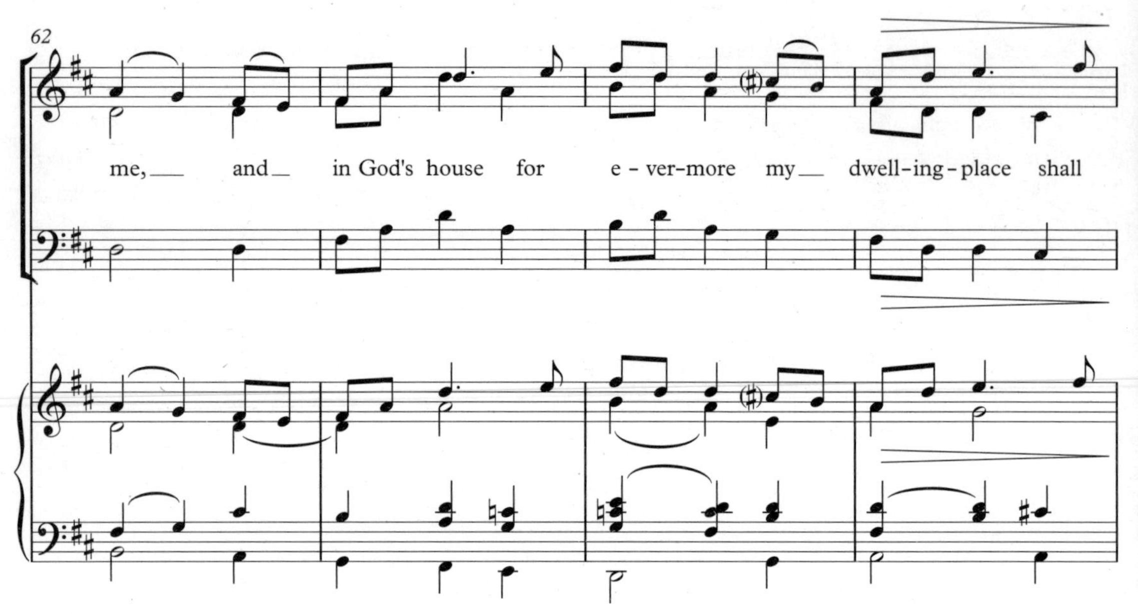
62
me, and in God's house for e - ver-more my dwell-ing-place shall

66
rit.
espress.
p
pp
be; and in God's house for e-ver-more my dwell-ing-place shall be.

14. Love bade me welcome

Words: GEORGE HERBERT (1593–1633)
from THE TEMPLE (1633)

Music: GEOFF WEAVER

12
p
near-er to me,
sweet-ly ques-tion-ing
if I lacked a-ny-thing.
p
p
15
mf
'A guest', I ans-wered, 'wor-thy to be here.'
mf
Man.
18
3
Love said,
'You shall be he.'
3
3
3
3
3
Ped.
Man.

21
SOPRANOS & ALTOS UNISON
mf
'I, the un-kind, un-grate-ful? Ah, my dear, I can-not look on thee.'
mp

24
Ped.

28
div. mp
Love took my hand, and smil - ing did re - ply,
mp

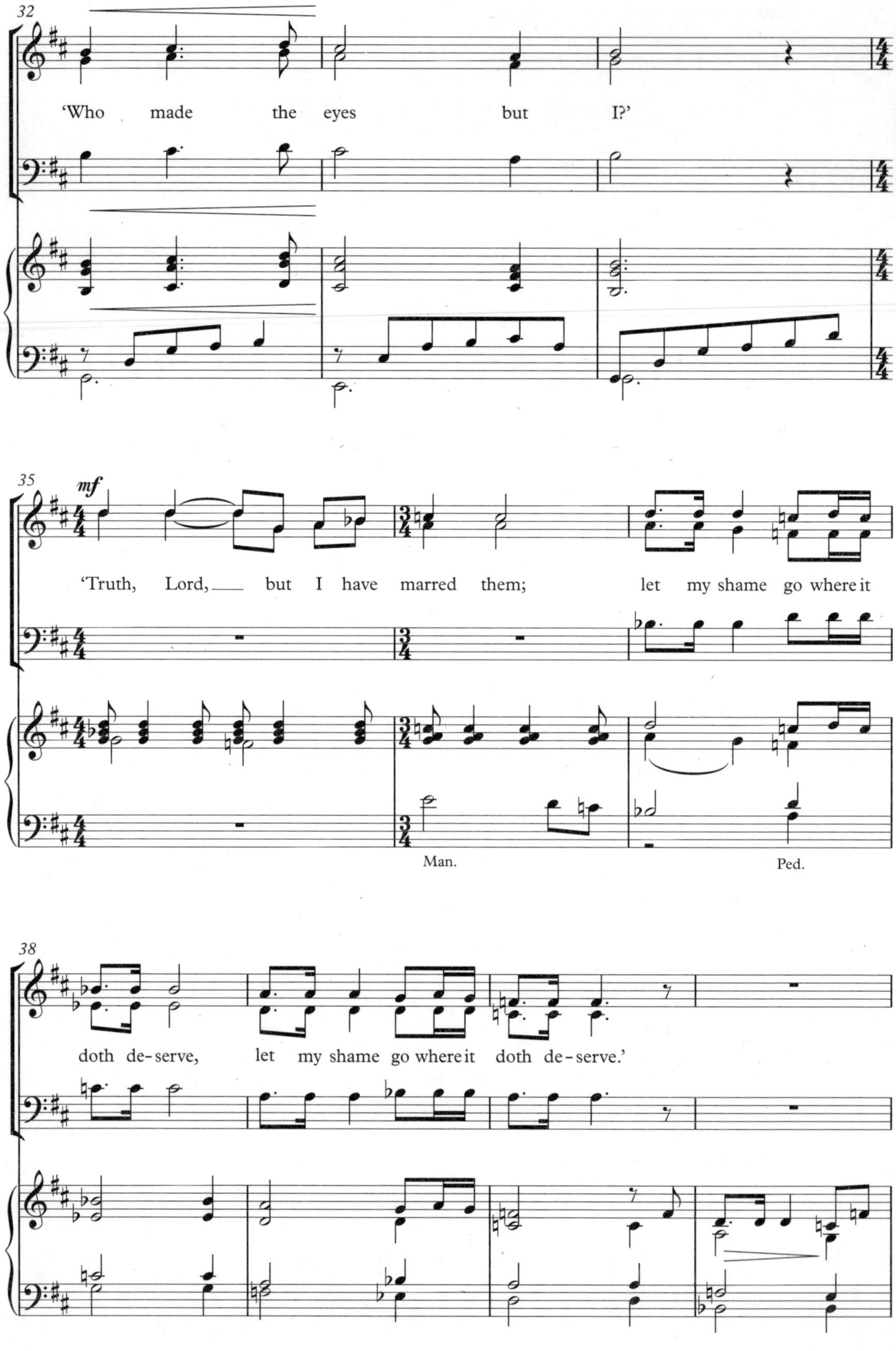

32

'Who made the eyes but I?'

35

mf

'Truth, Lord, __ but I have marred them; let my shame go where it

Man.

Ped.

42
p
'And know you not,' says Love, 'Who bore the blame?' 'My
p
p
47
3
dear, then I will serve.'
3
3
52
'You must sit down,' says Love, 'and taste my meat.'

57
mf
mp
rit.
So I did sit and eat, so I did sit and
mf
mp
rit.
mf
mp

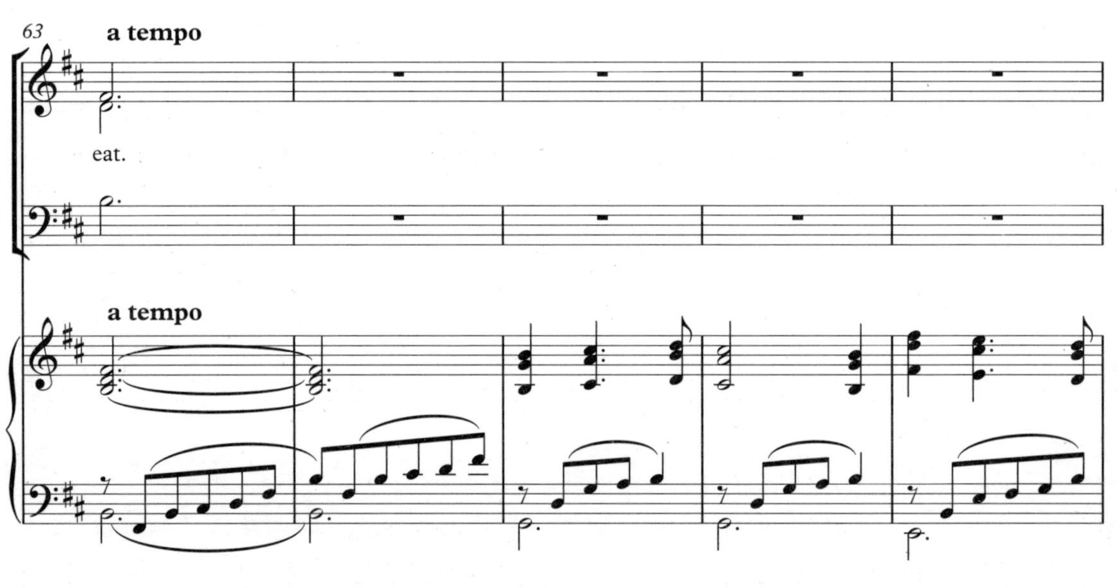
63
a tempo
eat.
a tempo

68

April 2012

15. Love Divine, all loves excelling

Words: CHARLES WESLEY (1707–1788) *Music:* AMY SUMMERS

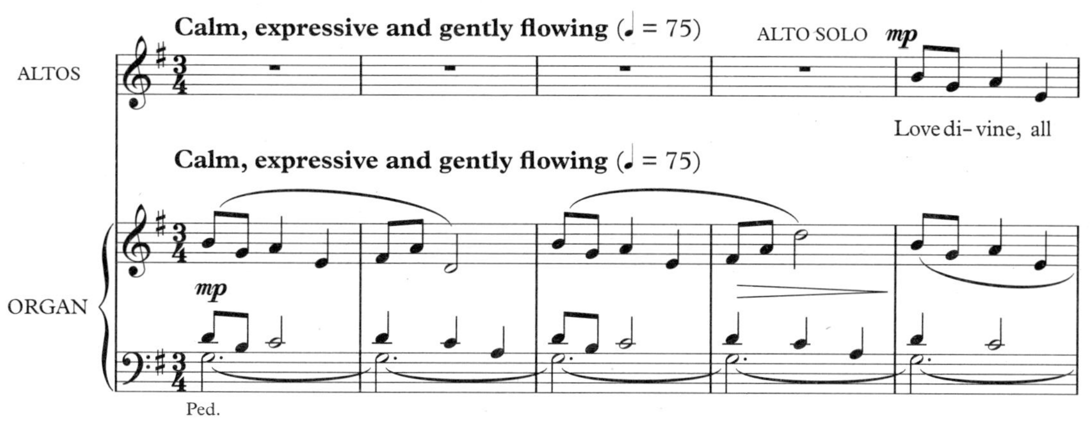

14
all com-pas - sion, pure un-boun - ded love thou art; vis - it us with

18
SOPRANOS & ALTOS (Full)
mp
thy sal - va - tion, en - ter ev - 'ery trem-bling heart. Love di - vine, all
MEN
mp
mp

22
loves ex - cel - ling, joy of heav'n, to earth come down, fix in us thy hum - ble

26
mp
dwell - ing, all thy faith - ful mer-cies crown. Je - su, thou art
mp
mp
30
all com - pas - sion, pure un - boun - ded love thou art; vis - it us with
34
p
thy sal - va - tion, en - ter ev - 'ry trem-bling heart.
p
p

38
mf
Come, al- migh - ty
mf
mp
42
to de - li - ver, let us all thy life re- ceive; sud - den - ly re -
f
f
f
46
mp
p
turn, and ne - ver, ne - ver more thy tem-ples leave. Thee we would be
mp
p
mp
p

50
SOPRANO
al-ways bles - sing, serve thee as thy hosts a-bove; pray, and praise thee,
ALTO
al-ways bles - sing, serve thee as thy hosts a-bove; pray, and praise thee,
MEN
al-ways bles - sing, serve thee as thy hosts a-bove; pray, and praise thee,
54
f
mf
with-out ceas-ing, glo-ry in thy per-fect love.
with-out ceas-ing, glo-ry in thy per-fect love.
with-out ceas-ing, glo-ry in thy per-fect love.
f

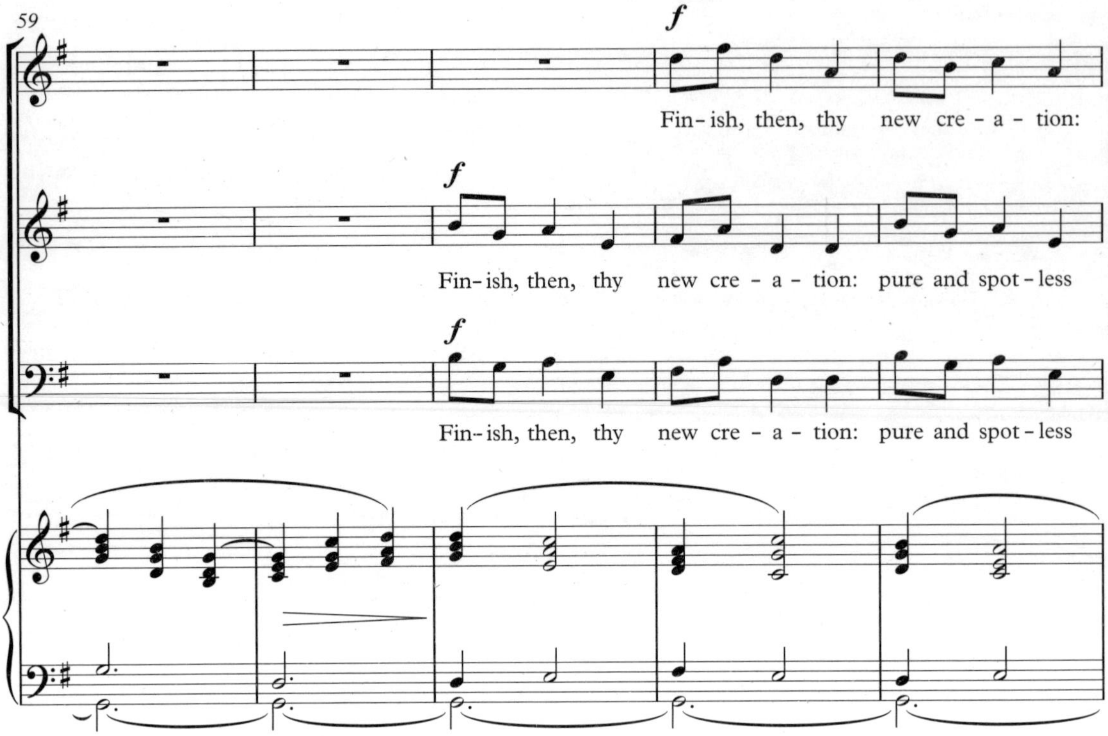
59
f
Fin-ish, then, thy new cre - a - tion:
f
Fin-ish, then, thy new cre - a - tion: pure and spot-less
f
Fin-ish, then, thy new cre - a - tion: pure and spot-less

64
let us be; per - fect-ly re -
let us be; let us see thy great sal - va - tion per-fect-ly re -
let us be; let us see thy great sal - va - tion per-fect-ly re -

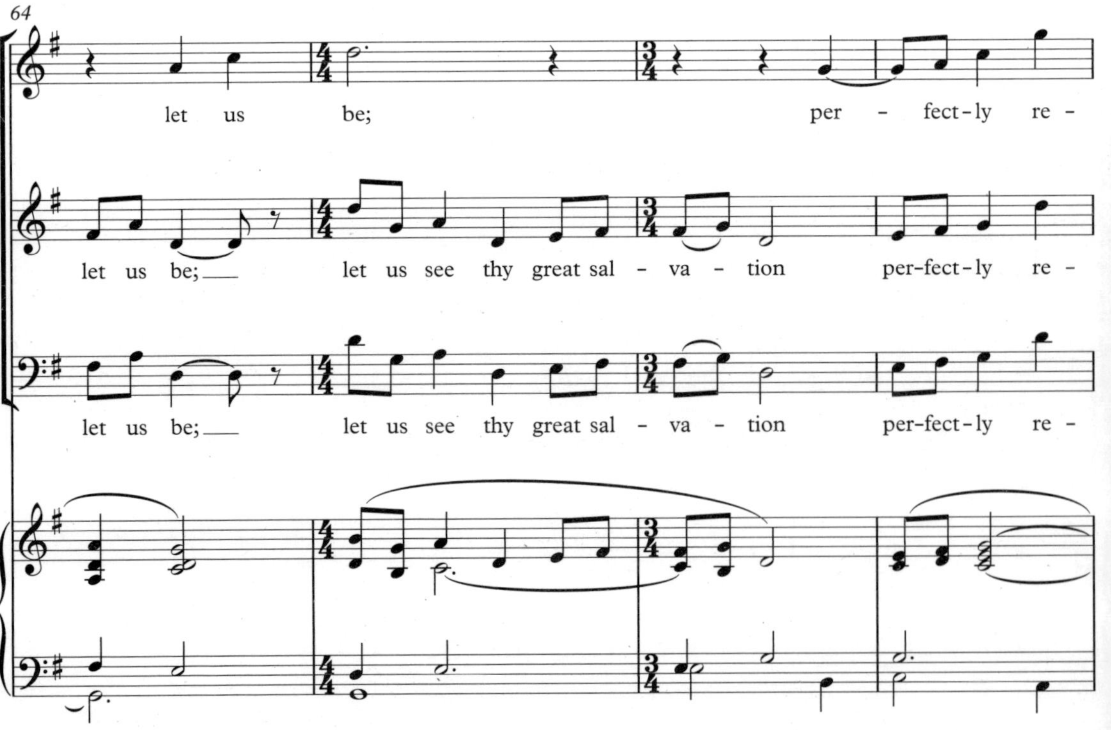

68
-stored in thee; Changed from glo - ry, till
-stored in thee; Changed from glo - ry in - to glo - ry, till in heav'n we
-stored in thee; Changed from glo - ry in - to glo - ry, till in heav'n we
72
ff
mf
in hea - ven, lost in won - der,
take our place, till we cast our crowns be - fore thee, lost in won - der,
take our place, till we cast our crowns be - fore thee, lost in won - der,

76

f

love, and praise, love, and praise, love, and praise,

f

love, and praise, love, and praise, love, and

f

love, and praise, love, and praise, love, and

f

81

f

rall. al fine

ff

love and praise, love, and praise!

ff

praise, love, and praise, love, and praise!

ff

praise, love, and praise, love, and praise!

rall. al fine

ff

for Annalisa

16. A Love Unfeigned

Words: GEOFFREY DEARMER (1893–1996) *Music:* THOMAS HEWITT JONES

12
woes to bear with - out thy help are we; can we each o - ther

16
bur - dens share, if we not bur - den thee, if we not bur - den thee?
mp
R.H.
p

21
UNISON mf
2. O won - der of the
mf
2. O won - der of the
p
mp

24
world with- stood! That night of prayer and doom was not the sun - set
world with- stood! That night of prayer and doom was not the sun - set

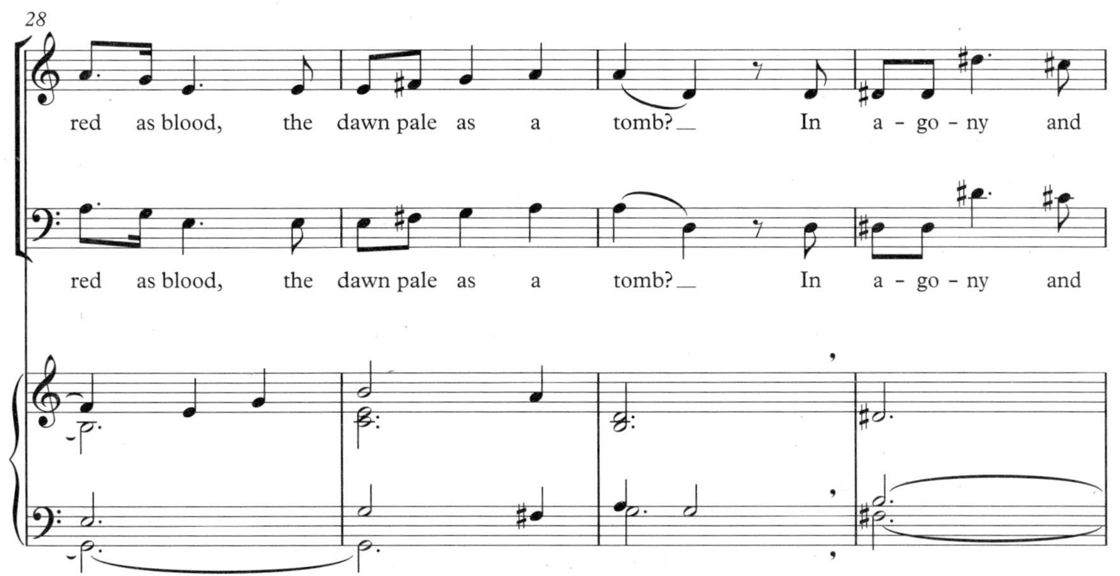
28
red as blood, the dawn pale as a tomb? In a - go - ny and
red as blood, the dawn pale as a tomb? In a - go - ny and

32
blood - y sweat, in tears of love un - feigned, O un - des - pair - ing
blood - y sweat, in tears of love un - feigned, O un - des - pair - ing
36
Lord, and yet, with man i - den - ti - fied, with man i - den - ti - fied.
Lord, and yet, with man i - den - ti - fied, with man i - den - ti - fied.
mp
cresc.
41
mf
mp
Man.

47
SOPRANOS
ALTOS
Ah
p
p
Ah
MEN
mp
3. As in dark drops the pit - ting rain falls on a dust - y
Solo (+ larigot
or similar)
mp
Sw.
p
Ped.

51
Ah
p
mp
so tears shall fall and fall a - gain to wash thy wound - ed
street, so tears shall fall and fall a - gain to wash thy wound - ed

55
mf sub.
f
feet. But thy quick hands to heal are strong, O love thy child - ren we, who
mf sub.
f
to Gt.
mf
(Gt.)
60
sing with joy the Pil - grim's song and walk, dear Lord, with thee, and
64
rit.
walk, dear Lord, with thee.
rit.
Solo *mp*
mp
sub. p
Sw.
p
pp
Sw.
Solo
(+32')

17. Morning glory, starlit sky

Words: WILLIAM HUBERT VANSTONE (1923–1999)

Music: GEOFF WEAVER

12
SOPRANO
ALTO
God, gifts of love to mind and sense;
MEN
O - pen are the gifts of God,
Man.
15
hid - den is love's a - go - ny,
p
poco rit.
hid - den is love, love's en - dea - vour, love's ex - pense.
p
poco rit.
p
Ped.
19
a tempo
mf
3. Love that gives, gives e - ver more,
gives with zeal, with ea - ger
mf
a tempo
mf
Man.
Ped.

22
hands. spares not, keeps not, all out - pours, ven-tures all, its all ex -
26
UNISON
p
pends. 4. Drained is love in mak-ing full, bound in set-ting o-thers
p
Man.
30
free, poor in mak-ing ma - ny rich, weak in giv - ing pow'r to
Ped.

34
div. mp
be.
5. There - fore he who shows us God hangs up-on the
mp
mp
38
mf
dim.
tree;
and the nails and crown of thorns tell of what God's love must
mf
dim.
mf
dim.
Man.
Ped.
rit.
a tempo
42
mf UNISON
be.
6. Here is God: no mo-narch he, throned in ea - sy state to
mf
rit.
a tempo
mf
Man.
Ped.

46
div.
mp
reign;
here is God, whose arms of love — ach - ing, spent, the
mp
mp
Man.
50
rit.
world sus - tain.
rit.

18. New Year Carol

Words: TRADITIONAL

Music: THOMAS HEWITT JONES

poco rit.
a tempo
mf
f
15
wa - ter and the wine, the se - ven bright gold wires, and the
mf
f
poco rit.
a tempo
mf
f

19
mp
p
bu - gles that do shine.
mp
p
mp
mf

24

SOPRANOS

mf

Sing_ reign of fair maid with_ gold up-on her toe, o-pen

ALTOS

mf

Sing reign of_ gold up on her toe,_ o-pen

MEN

mf

Sing_ reign of fair maid with_ gold up-on her toe, o-pen

mp

29

f *mf*

you the west door, and turn the old year go, sing_ le-vy-dew, sing

f *mf* *f*

you the west door,_ and turn the old year go, sing le-vy-dew, sing

f *mf*

you the west door, and turn the old year go,_ sing le-vy-dew, sing

mf *f* *mf*

34
poco rit.
a tempo
f
ff
le - vy - dew, the wa - ter and the wine, the se - ven bright gold wires, and the
le - vy - dew, the wa - ter and the wine, the se - ven bright gold wires, and the
le - vy - dew, the wa - ter and the wine, the se - ven bright gold wires, and the
poco rit.
a tempo
39
mf
mp
bu - gles that do shine.
bu - gles that do shine.
bu - gles that do shine.

44

f

Ah, ___

f

Sing_ reign of fair maid with gold u-pon her

f

Sing_ reign of fair maid with gold u-pon her

f

48

__ ah, ___

chin, o-pen you__ the east door, and let the new year

chin, o-pen you the east door, and_ let the new year

molto rit.
52
(f)
sing le - vy - dew, sing le - vy - dew, the wa - ter and the
in, sing le - vy - dew, sing le - vy - dew, the wa - ter and the
in, sing le - vy - dew, sing le - vy - dew, the wa - ter and the
molto rit.
a tempo
(slightly slower than opening)
56
ff
f
mf
wine, the se - ven bright gold wires, and the
wine, the se - ven bright gold wires, and the
wine, the se - ven bright gold wires, and the
a tempo
(slightly slower than opening)

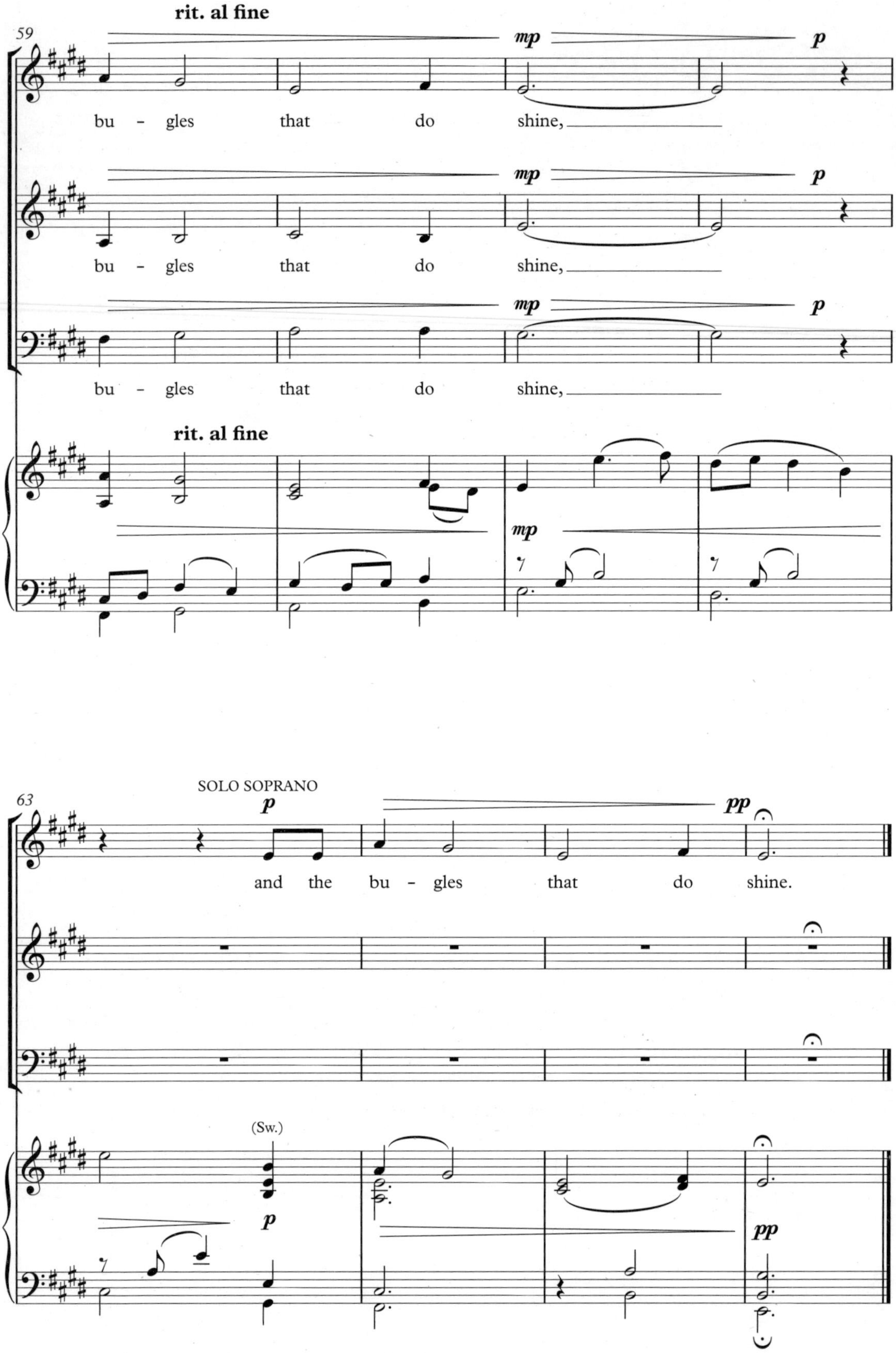

rit. al fine

59

mp *p*

bu - gles that do shine,

mp *p*

bu - gles that do shine,

mp *p*

bu - gles that do shine,

rit. al fine

mp

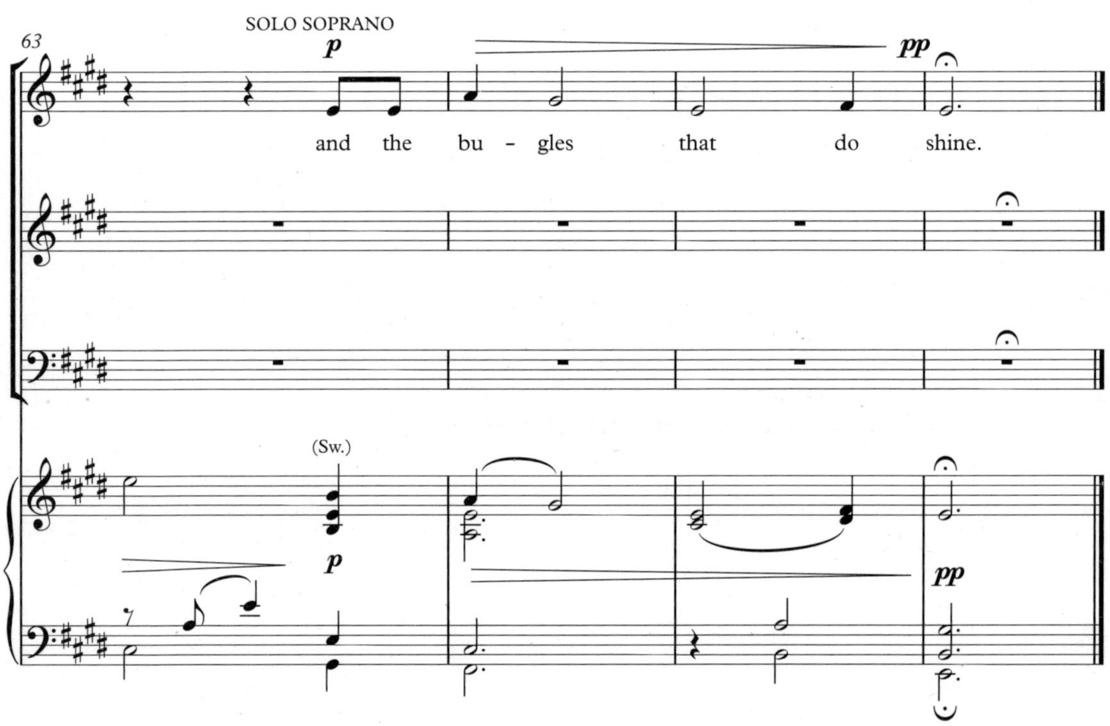

19. Nunc Dimittis

Words: The Book of Common Prayer

Music: Plainchant (Tone V)
and Toby Young

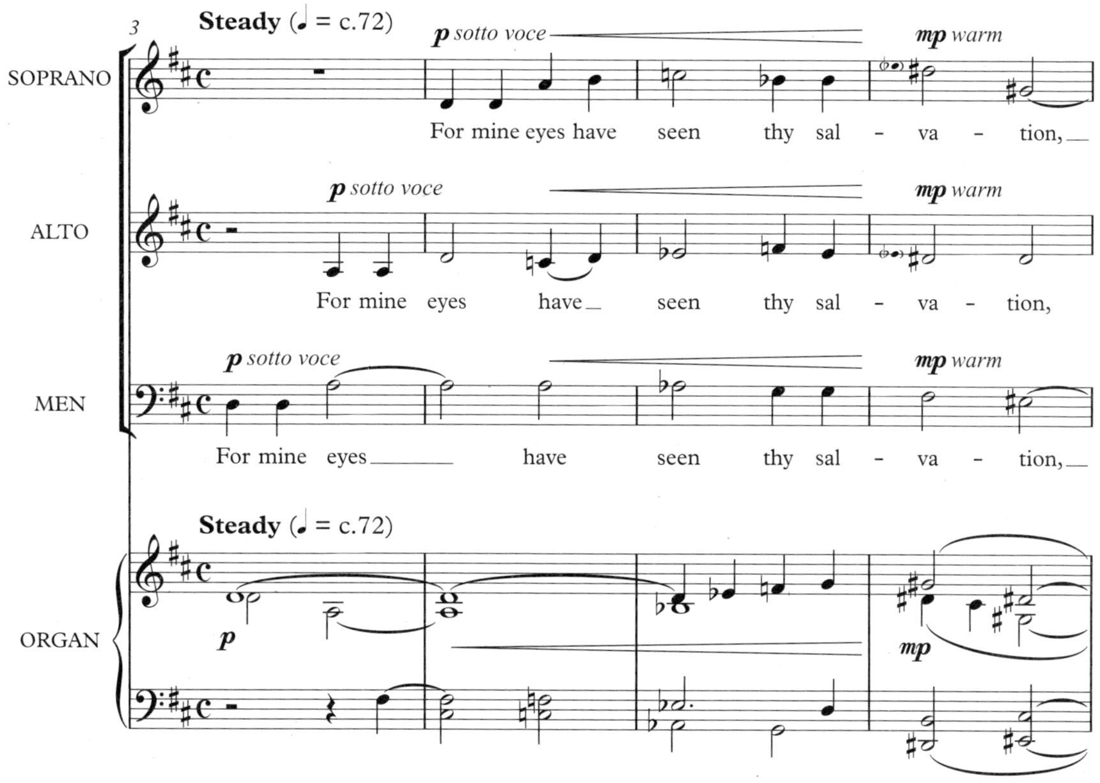

3 **Steady** (♩ = c.72)

SOPRANO — *p sotto voce* — *mp warm*
For mine eyes have seen thy sal - va - tion,___

ALTO — *p sotto voce* — *mp warm*
For mine eyes have_ seen thy sal - va - tion,

MEN — *p sotto voce* — *mp warm*
For mine eyes_______ have seen thy sal - va - tion,___

Steady (♩ = c.72)

ORGAN — *p* — *mp*

7
mf ma non troppo
which thou hast pre - pared be -
mf ma non troppo
which thou hast pre - pared be - fore the
mf ma non troppo
which thou hast pre -
mf
11
p dolciss.
- fore the face of all peo - - ple.
p dolciss.
face, the face of all peo - ple.
p dolciss.
- pared be - fore the face of all peo - ple.
p
16
SOPRANOS & ALTOS
To be a light to light - en the Gen-tiles and to be the glo - ry of thy peo-ple Is - ra - el.

18 **As before**

mp cantabile *mf*

Glo - ry be ___ to the Fa - ther, ___

mp cantabile *mf*

Glo - ry be, glo - ry be to the Fa - ther,

mp cantabile *mf*

Glo - ry be, ___ glo - ry be to the Fa - ther, ___

As before

mp *mf*

22 *poco a poco cresc.*

___ and to the Son, ___ and ___

poco a poco cresc.

and to the Son, ___ and ___ to ___ the

cresc.

___ and to the Son, and

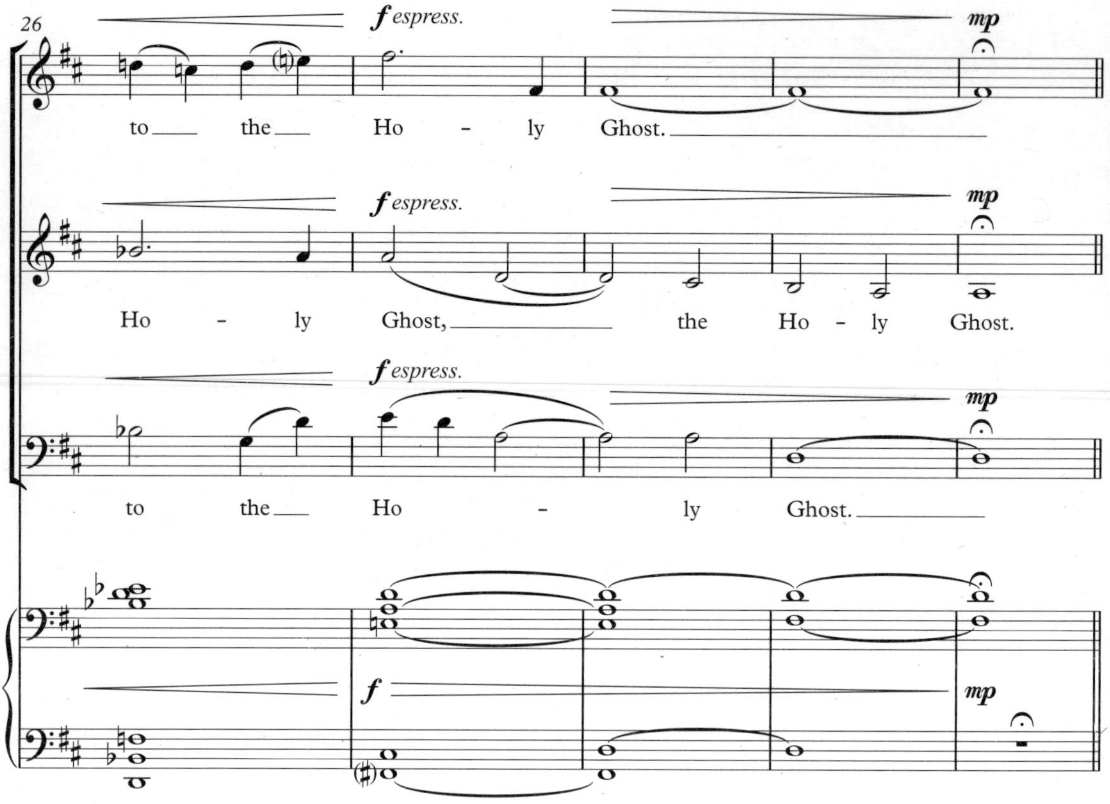
26
f espress.
mp
to the Ho - ly Ghost.
f espress.
mp
Ho - ly Ghost, the Ho - ly Ghost.
f espress.
mp
to the Ho - ly Ghost.
f
mp

31
MEN
As it was in the beginning, is now and e - ver shall be, world with-out end. A - men.

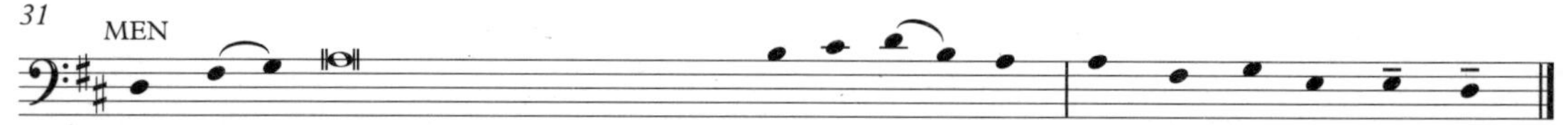

20. O be joyful in the Lord

Words: Psalm 100

Music: Ian Carpenter

* If the 'Men' part is too low for some singers, the alternative small notes may be sung.

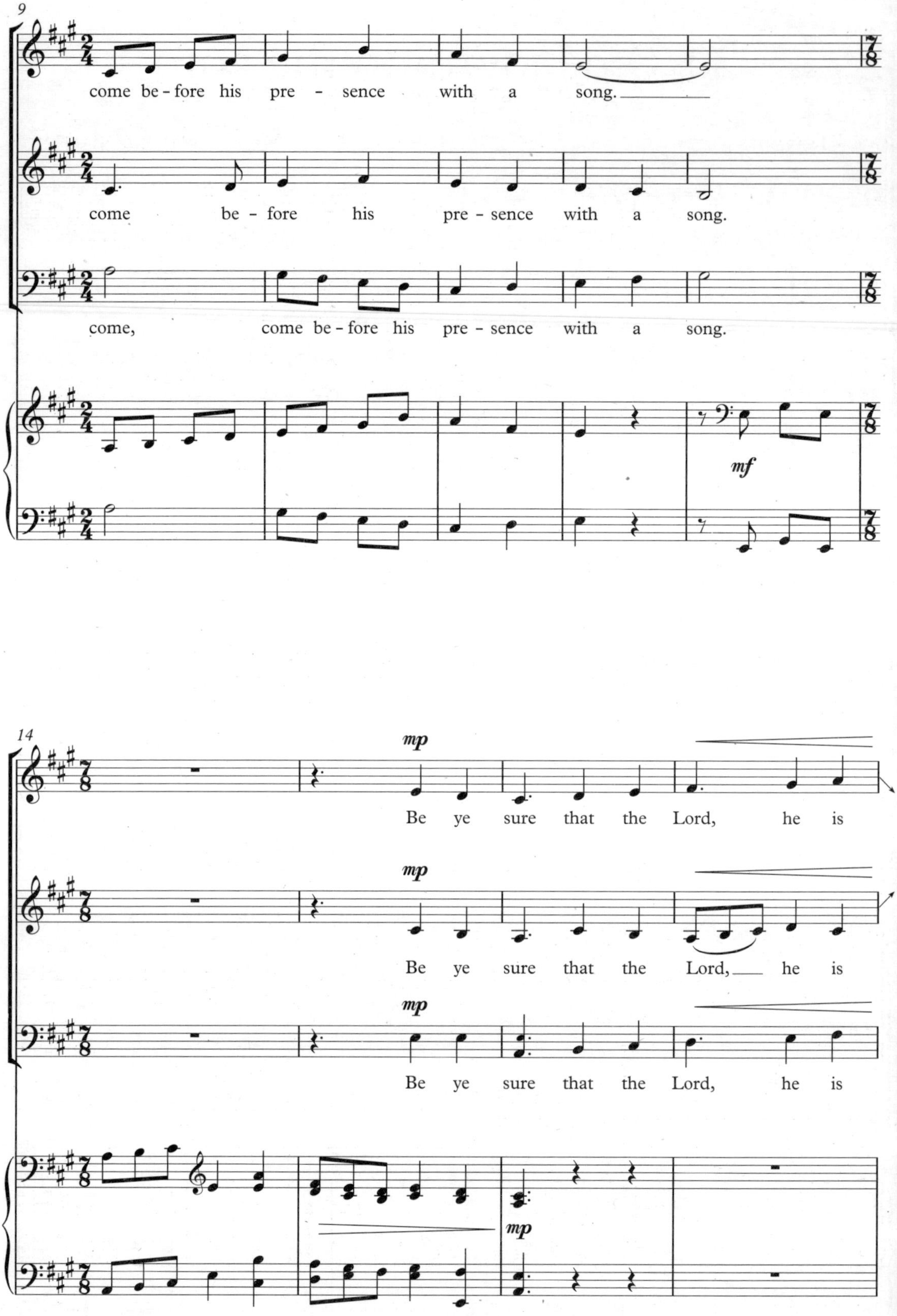

14

mp

Be ye sure that the Lord, he is

mp

Be ye sure that the Lord, he is

mp

Be ye sure that the Lord, he is

mp

SOPRANOS & ALTOS
18
mf
God, it is he that has made us and
mf
mf
(Ped.)
22
not we our - selves,
26
f
we are his peo - ple and the
f
f
(Man.)

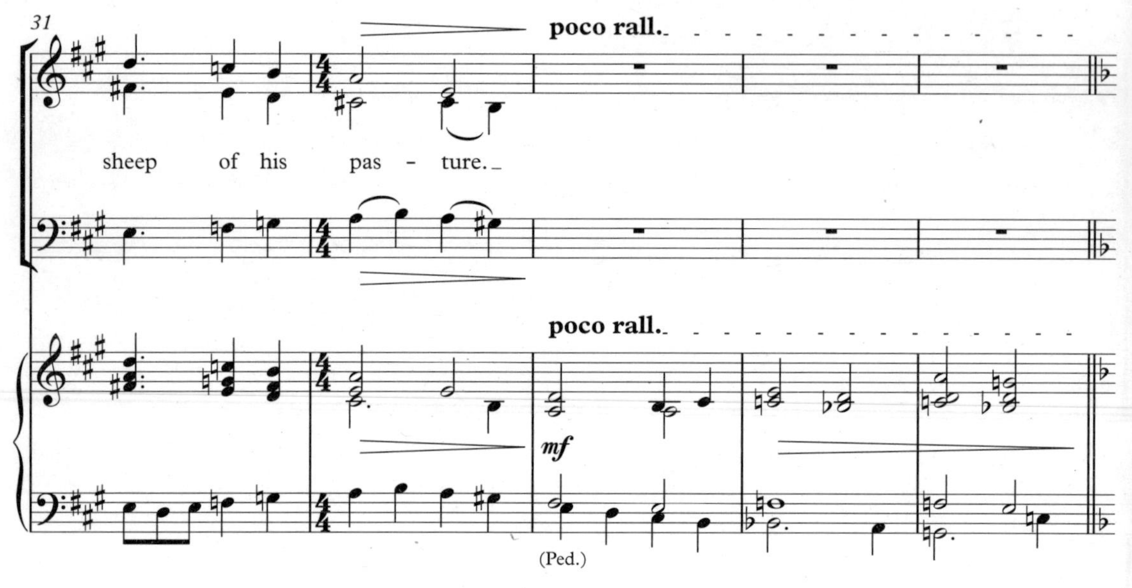
31
poco rall.
sheep of his pas - ture.
poco rall.
mf
(Ped.)

36
Tranquil (♩ = 96)
SOPRANOS mp espress.
O go your
Tranquil (♩ = 96)
mp

41
way in - to his gates with thanks - giv - ing,

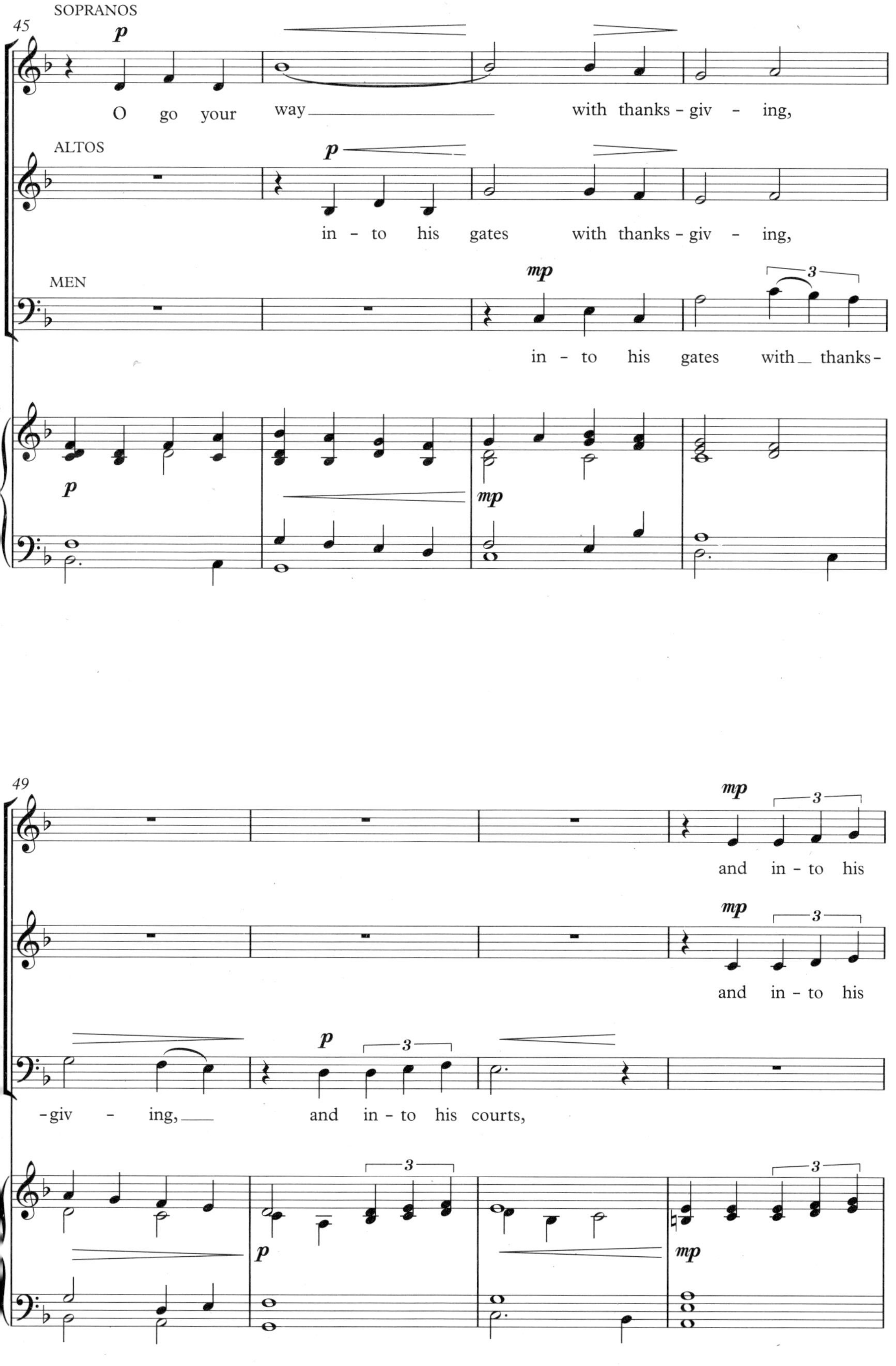

45

SOPRANOS

p

O go your way ______ with thanks - giv - ing,

ALTOS

p

in - to his gates with thanks - giv - ing,

MEN

mp

in - to his gates with __ thanks-

p

mp

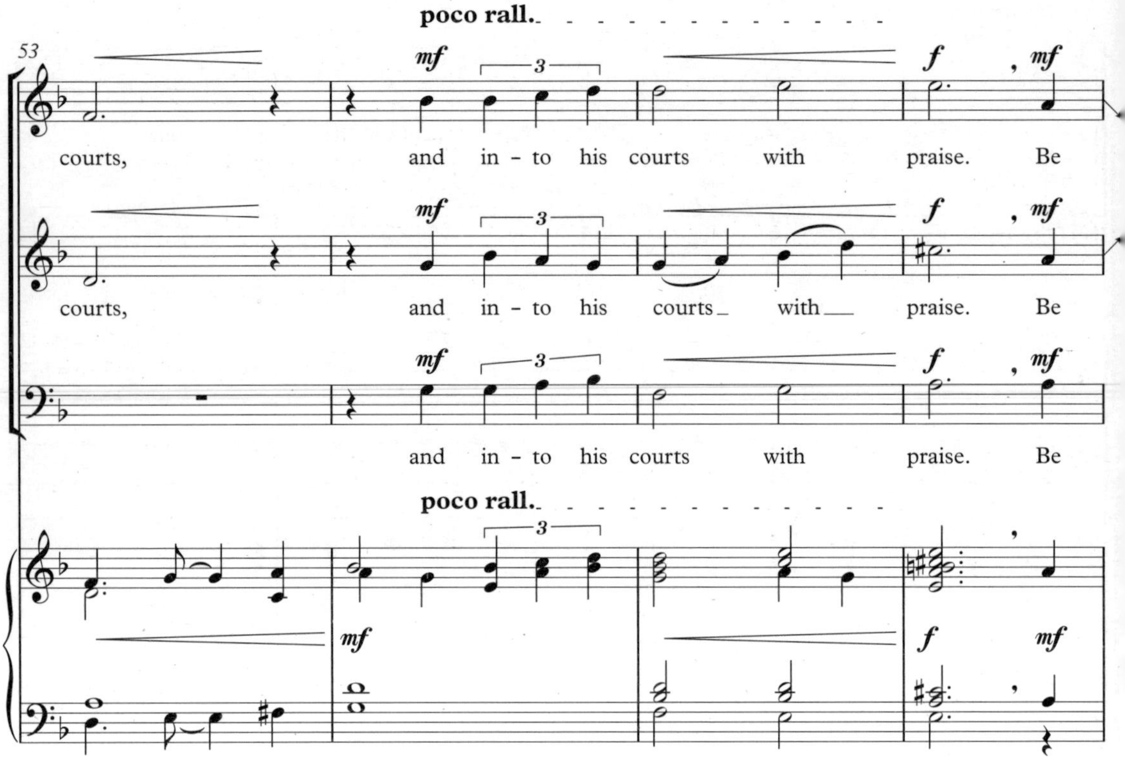
poco rall.
53
mf
f
mf
courts, and in - to his courts with praise. Be
courts, and in - to his courts with praise. Be
and in - to his courts with praise. Be
poco rall.
mf
f
mf

SOPRANOS & ALTOS
Slightly slower (♩ = 92)
57
mp
thank - ful un - to him, and speak good of his Name.
mp
Slightly slower (♩ = 92)
mp

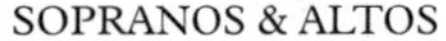

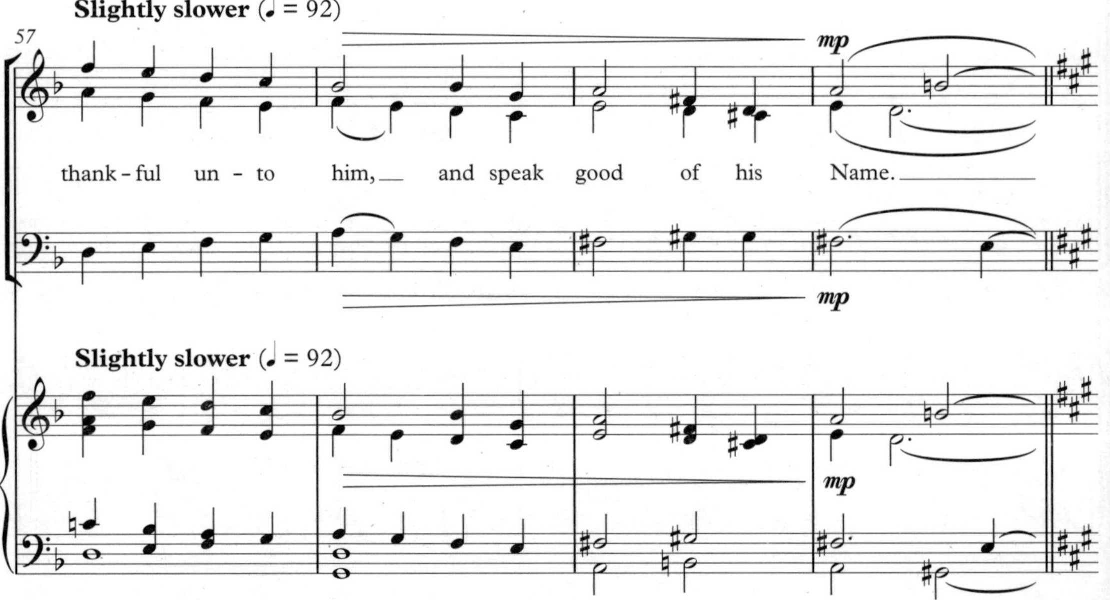

61
p legato
For the Lord is gracious, his mercy is ever-
p legato
(Optional acc.)
p
(Man.)
65
mp
-lasting, and his truth endureth from
mp
mp
69
poco rall.
p
generation to generation.
p
poco rall.
p

73

Lively, as before (♩. = 108)

f

Glo - ry be — to the

f

Lively, as before (♩. = 108)

f

(Man.)

77

Fa - ther and to the Son and to — the Ho - ly

81

mf *mp*

Ghost, as it was in the be - gin - ning, is

mf *mp*

mf *mp*

(Ped.)

Bristol, 8th April 2018

21. O for a closer walk with God

Words: WILLIAM COWPER (1732–1800)

Music: THOMAS HEWITT JONES

12
mp
2. The dear - est_ i- dol
mp
Man.
Ped.
16
SOPRANOS & ALTOS
mp
2. The dear - est_ i- dol I have known, what-e'er that i - dol
(MEN)
I have known, what - e'er that i - dol
p
19
be, help me to tear it from thy throne, and wor-ship on-ly

23
thee.
p
Man.
Ped.

27
p
3. So shall my walk be close with God,
p
3. So shall my walk be close with God, calm and se-
mp
p

30
calm and se - rene my frame; So pur - er light shall
- rene my frame; So pur - er light shall

33
rit.
Slow and poignant
molto rit.
p
pp a niente
mark the road that leads me to the Lamb.
p
pp a niente
rit.
Slow and poignant
molto rit.
p
pp a niente
Man.

To Dr Phillip McCarthy on the occasion of the opening of the Health Centre in Westbury on Trym, Bristol September 2008

22. Prayer of Saint Teresa

Words: Saint Teresa

Music: David Ogden

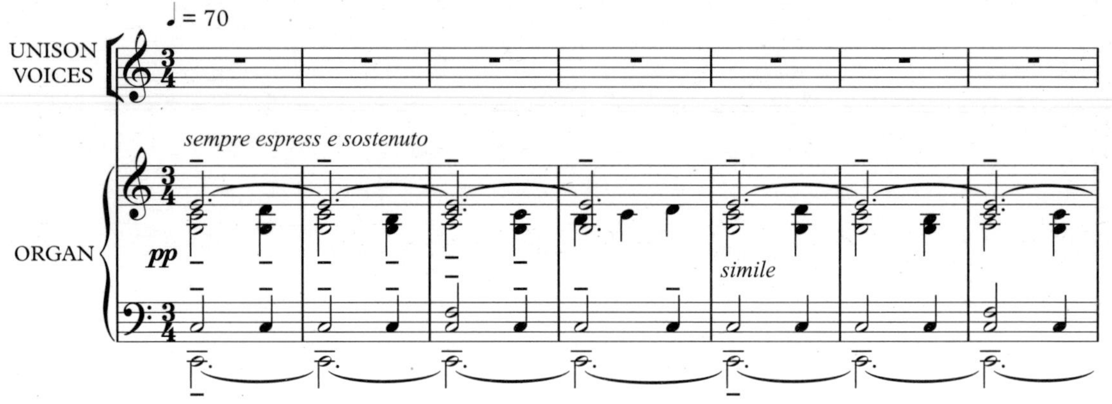

18
3
not for - get the in - fi - nite pos - si - bi - li - ties born of

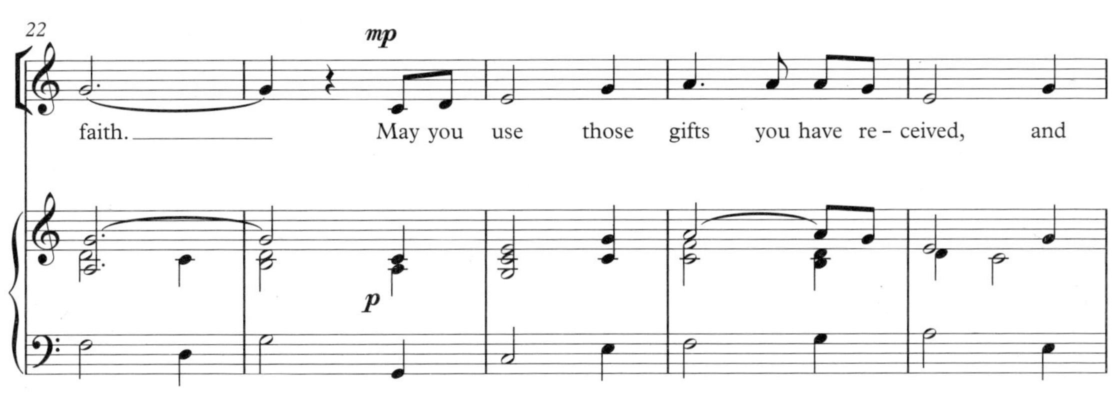
22
mp
faith. May you use those gifts you have re - ceived, and
p

27
mf
pass on the love that has been giv - en to you. May you
mp

37
pp sotto voce
p
— Let this pre-sence set-tle in - to your bones, and al - low your
pp

47
love, to sing, to dance, to praise and love.
love, to sing, to dance, to praise and love.

poco rit.
52
mp
UNISON
p
It is there for each and every one of us, it is
p
mp
It is there for each and every one of us, it is
poco rit.
p
p

57
SOPRANOS & ALTOS
there for each and ev - ery one of us it is
there for each and ev - ery one of us
pp

62
poco rall.
there for each and ev - ery one of us.
poco rall.

for my wonderful foster father, Richard Abbott, and the parish choir of Bisley & West End, Surrey

23. Saint Richard's Prayer

Words: Ascribed to St Richard of Chichester (1197–1253)

Music: Joanna Forbes L'Estrange

9

be - ne - fits which thou hast won for us; Thanks be to

13

thee, Lord Je - sus Christ, for all the

17

div. *mf cresc.*

pains and in - sults thou hast borne for us; O most

mf cresc.

mf cresc.

21
poco f
mer - ci - ful Re - deem - er, friend and bro - ther, Sa - viour,
poco f
poco f
26
poco rit.
f
a tempo
hear our prayer: May we know thee more clear - ly, may we
f
hear our prayer: May we know thee more clear - ly,
poco rit.
a tempo
f
31
mf
love thee more dear - ly, and fol - low thee more near - ly, day by
mf
love thee more dear - ly, and fol - low thee more near - ly, day by
mf

36
f
mf
day. May we know thee more clear - ly, may we love thee more dear - ly, and
day. May we know thee more clear - ly, love thee more dear - ly, and
41
mp
fol - low thee more near - ly, day by day.
fol - low thee more near - ly, day by day.
46
mf espress.
Thanks be to thee, Lord Je - sus Christ
mp

51
for all the be - ne - fits which thou hast won for
55
us;
Thanks be to thee, Lord Je - sus Christ, for all the
60
mf cresc.
O most
pains and in - sults thou hast borne for us;
mf cresc.
mf cresc.

64
poco f
mer - ci - ful Re - deem - er, friend and bro - ther, Sa - viour,
poco f
poco f
69
f
hear our prayer: May we know thee more clear - ly, may we
f
hear our prayer: May we know thee more clear - ly,
f
74
mf
love thee more dear - ly, and fol - low thee more near - ly, day by
mf
love thee more dear - ly, and fol - low thee more near - ly day by
mf

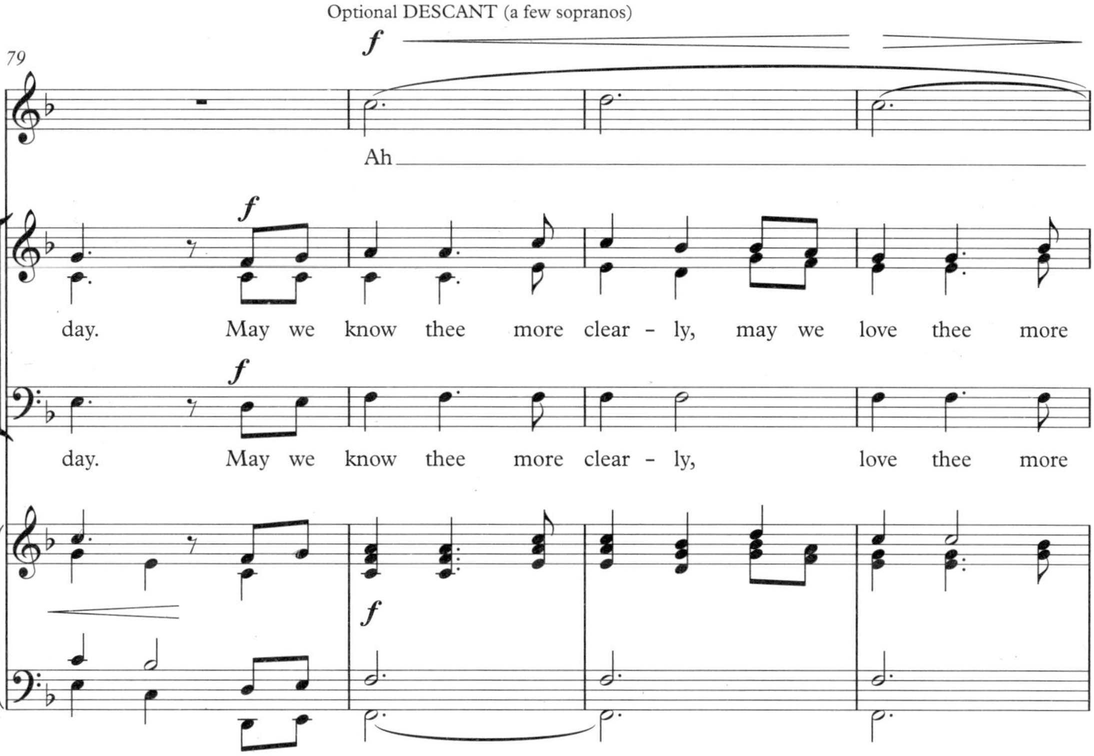

Optional DESCANT (a few sopranos)

79

Ah

day. May we know thee more clear - ly, may we love thee more

day. May we know thee more clear - ly, love thee more

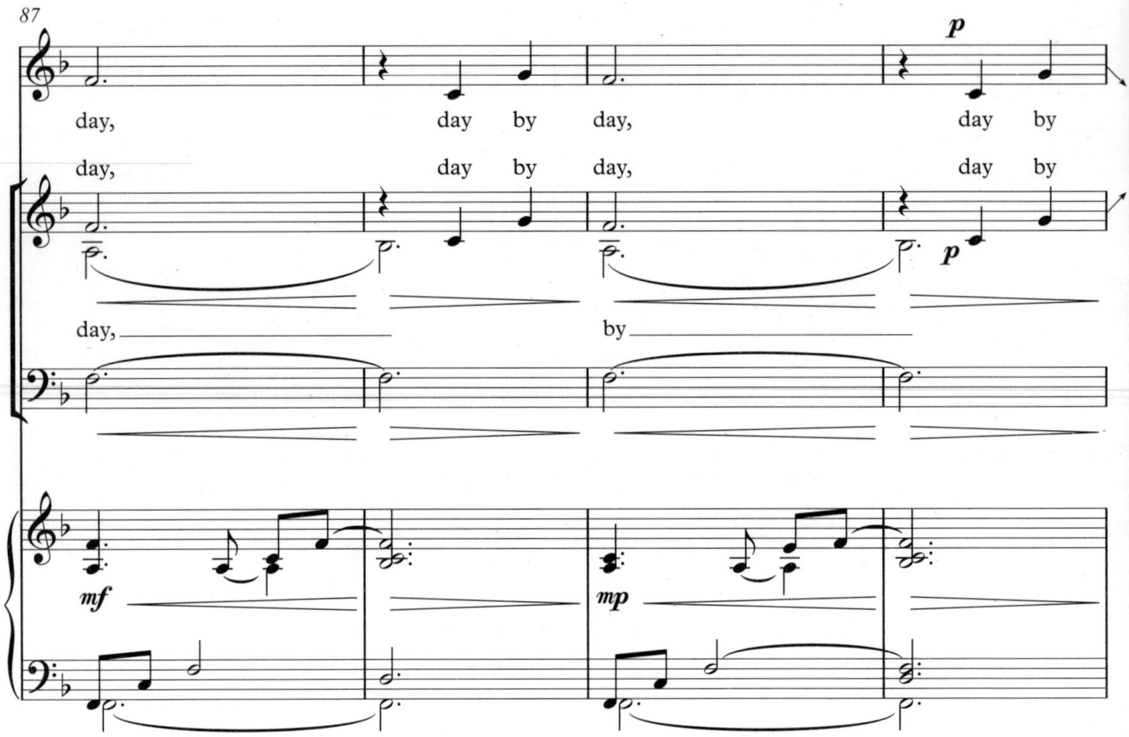
87
p
day, day by day, day by
day, day by day, day by
p
day, by
mf
mp

91
p
pp
day. A - men.
p
pp
p
pp

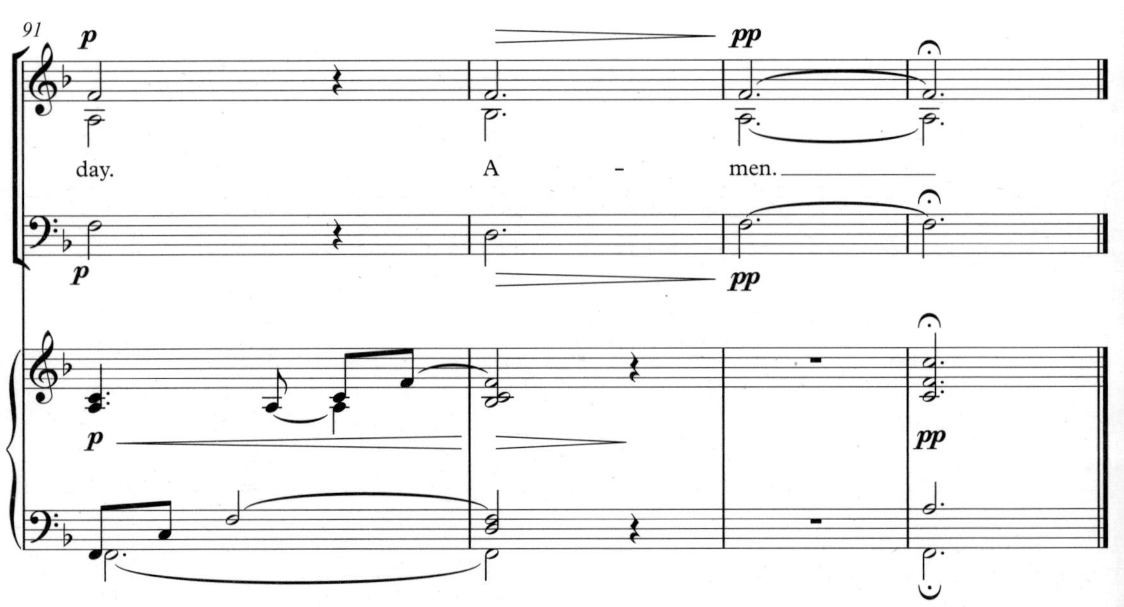

24. Thine be the glory

Words: EDMOND BUDRY (1854–1932)
translated by RICHARD BIRCH HOYLE (1875–1939)

Music: ALAN BULLARD

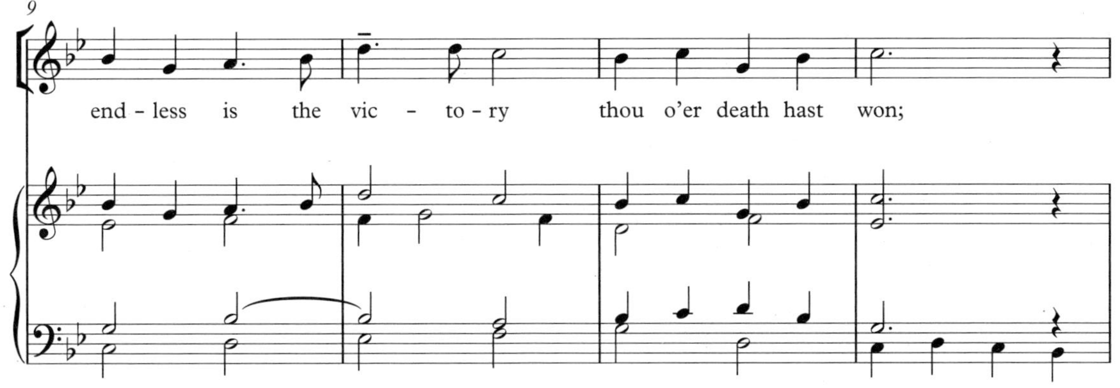

SOPRANOS & ALTOS

13 *mf*

an - gels in bright rai - ment rolled the stone a - way,

MEN *mf*

an - gels in bright rai - ment rolled the stone a - way,

mf

17 *cresc.* *f*

kept the fold - ed grave - clothes where thy bo - dy lay.

cresc. *f*

cresc. *f*

21 *ff*

Thine be the glo - ry, ri - sen, con-qu'ring Son,

ff

ff

* Piano may omit the small notes

25
end - less is the vic - t'ry thou o'er death hast won.
29
dim.
33
p espress.
2. Lo, Je - sus meets us, ri - sen from the tomb;
p espress.
Man.

37

poco a poco cresc.

lov - ing - ly he greets us, scat - ters fear and gloom;

poco a poco cresc.

Let the church with glad - ness hymns of tri - umph sing,

41

f

Let the church with glad - ness hymns of tri - umph sing,

f

Let the church with glad - ness hymns of tri - umph sing, for her

f

Ped.

45

for her Lord now liv - eth, death hath lost its sting.

Lord now liv - eth, death hath lost its sting.

49
Thine be the glo - ry, ri - sen, con-qu'ring Son,
53
end - less is the vic - t'ry thou o'er death hast won.
mf
57
poco a poco cresc.
61
f

66
SOPRANOS
f
3. No more we doubt thee, glo - rious Prince of
ALTOS
f
3. No more we doubt thee, glo - rious Prince of Life;
MEN
f
3. No more we doubt thee, glo - rious Prince of Life;

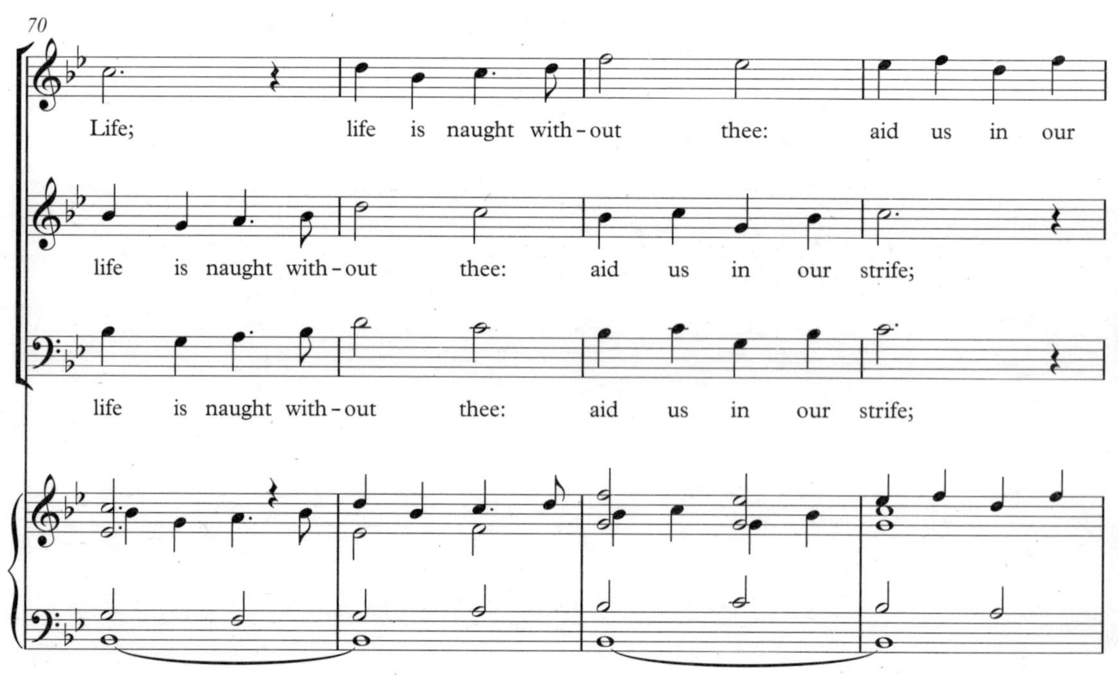
70
Life; life is naught with - out thee: aid us in our
life is naught with - out thee: aid us in our strife;
life is naught with - out thee: aid us in our strife;

74
strife; make us more than con-qu'rors through thy love;
make us more than con - que-rors through thy death-less love;
make us more than con - que - rors through thy death-less love;

78
cresc.
ff
bring us safe through Jor - dan to thy home a - bove:
cresc.
ff
bring us safe through Jor - dan to thy home a - bove:
cresc.
ff
bring us safe through Jor - dan to thy home a - bove:
cresc.
ff

82
SOPRANOS & ALTOS
Thine be the glo - ry, ri - sen, con - qu'ring Son, end - less is the
MEN
87
vic - t'ry, end - less is the vic - 'try thou o'er death hast
Reeds
92
fff
won.
fff
Full
fff

25. Thou knowest, Lord

Words: THE BOOK OF COMMON PRAYER (1662)
from THE ORDER FOR THE BURIAL OF THE DEAD

Music: OWAIN PARK

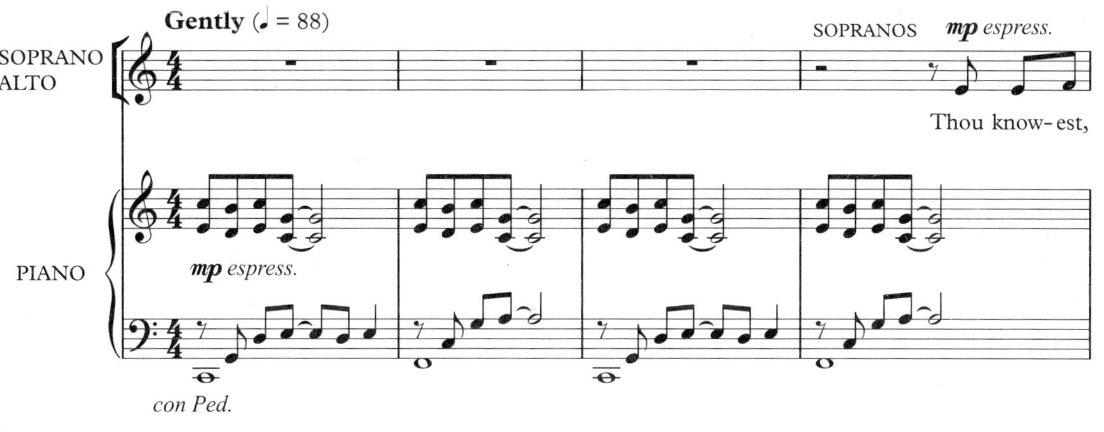

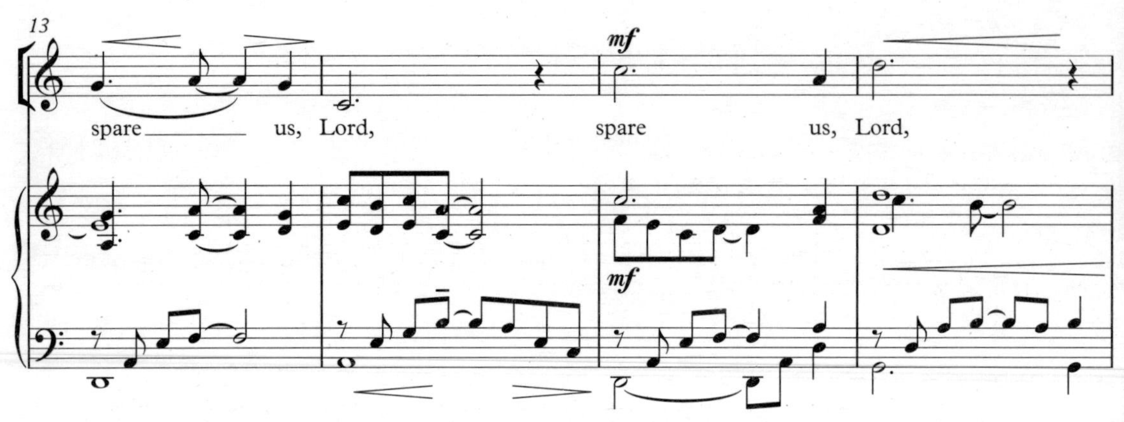
13
mf
spare us, Lord, spare us, Lord,
mf

17
f
spare us, Lord most ho - ly,
f
mp dim.

(SOPRANOS)
SOPRANOS & ALTOS
21
mf
mp
p
ho - ly, ho - ly, ho - ly,
MEN p
mp
ho - ly, O God most
pp
p

25
ALTOS mp
O ho - ly and most mer - ci-ful Sa - viour, thou most
mp
migh - ty, O ho - ly and most mer - ci - ful Sa - viour, thou most
mp

29
wor - thy judge e - ter - nal,
wor - thy judge e - ter - nal,

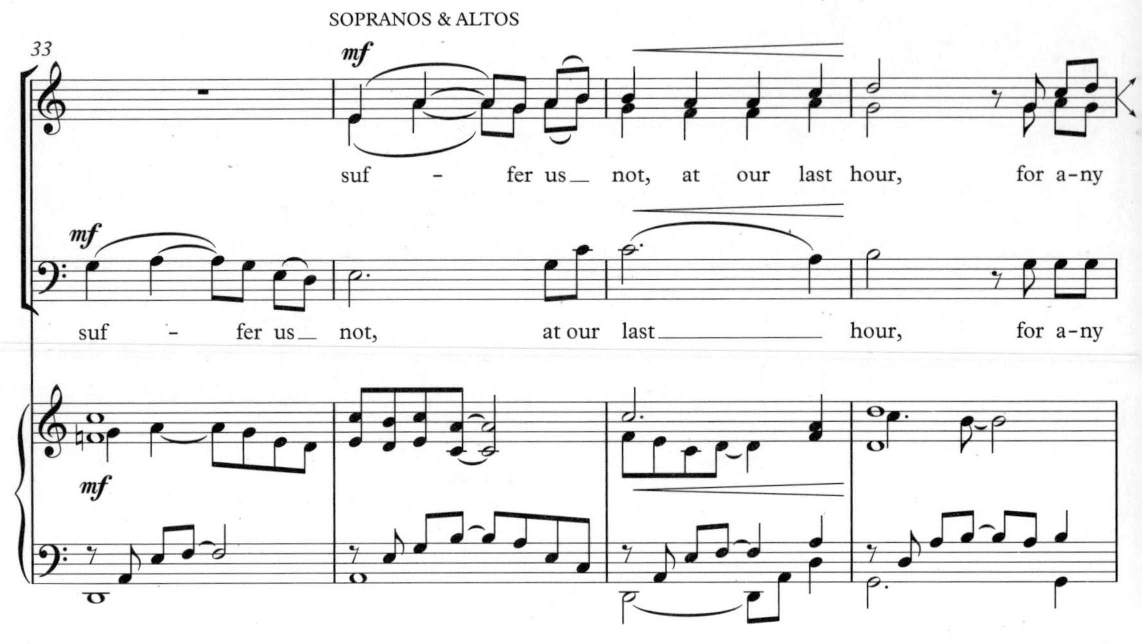

SOPRANOS & ALTOS
33
mf
suf - fer us not, at our last hour, for a-ny
mf
suf - fer us not, at our last hour, for a-ny
mf

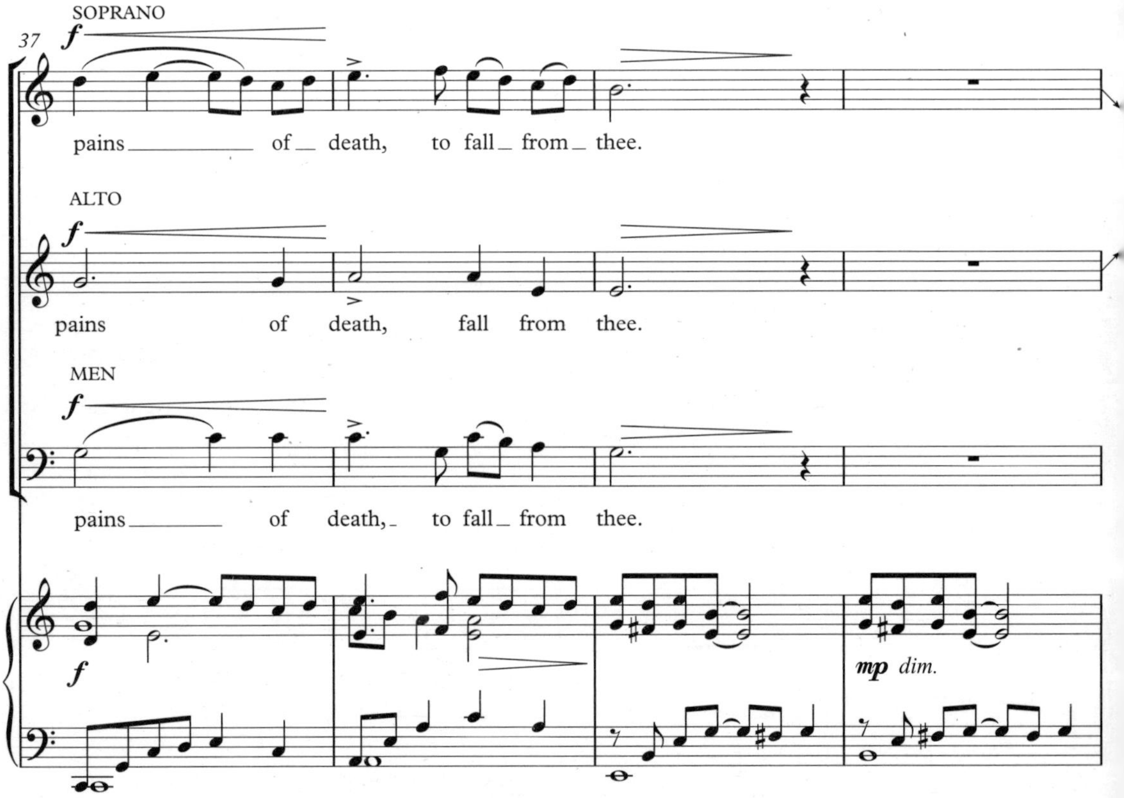
SOPRANO
37
f
pains of death, to fall from thee.
ALTO
f
pains of death, fall from thee.
MEN
f
pains of death, to fall from thee.
f
mp dim.

41
mp
ho - ly,
ho - ly,
ho - ly,
mp
poco a poco dim.

45
UNISON
mp
Thou know- est,
mp
p espress.
mp

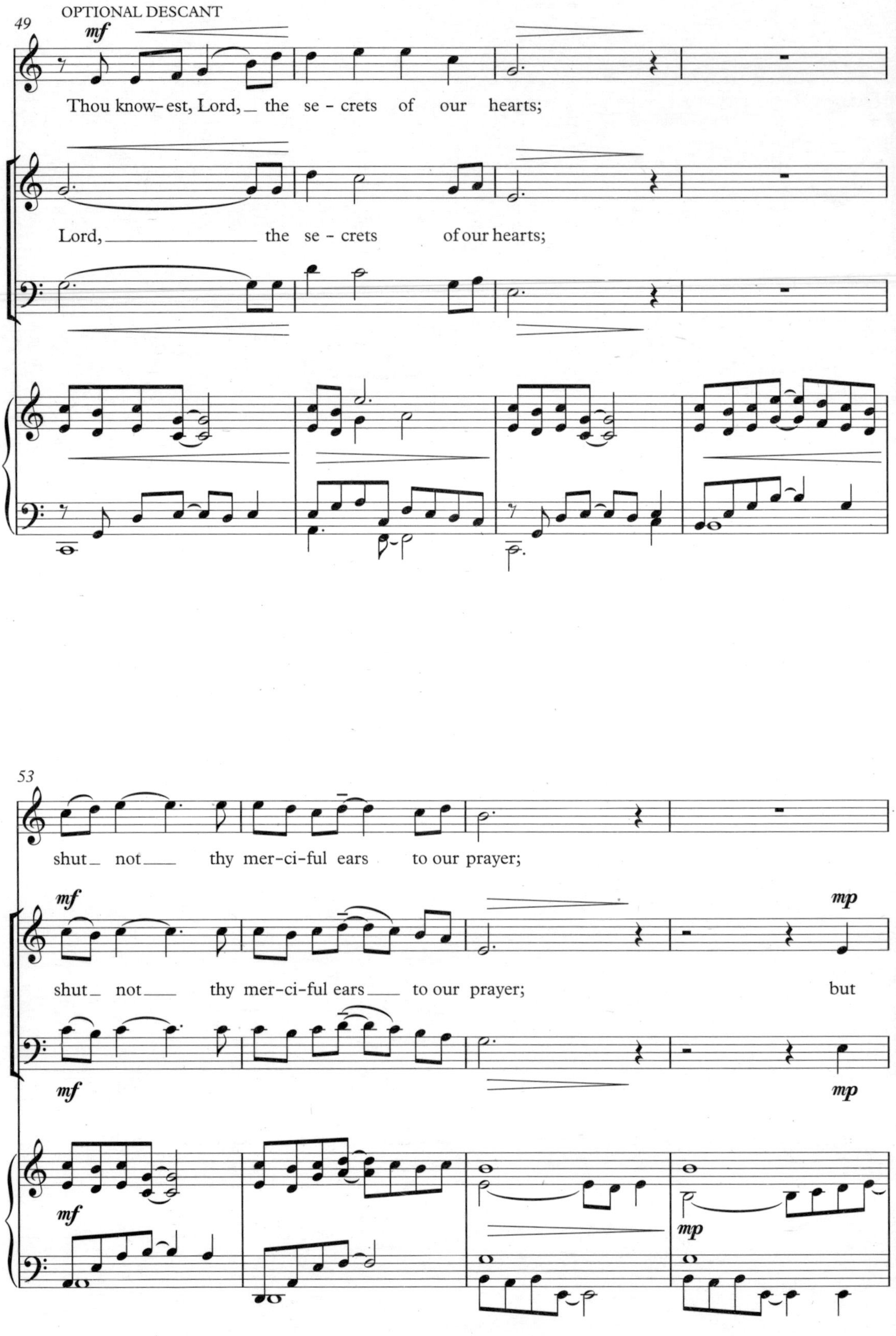

49 OPTIONAL DESCANT
mf
Thou know-est, Lord, the se-crets of our hearts;
Lord, the se-crets of our hearts;

57
mf
spare us, Lord, spare us,
div. mf
spare us, Lord, spare us, Lord,
mf
mf
(DESCANT)
61
f
Lord, most ho - ly,
SOPRANO
f
spare us, Lord most ho - ly,
ALTO
f
spare us, Lord most ho - ly,
MEN
f
spare us, Lord most ho - ly,
f

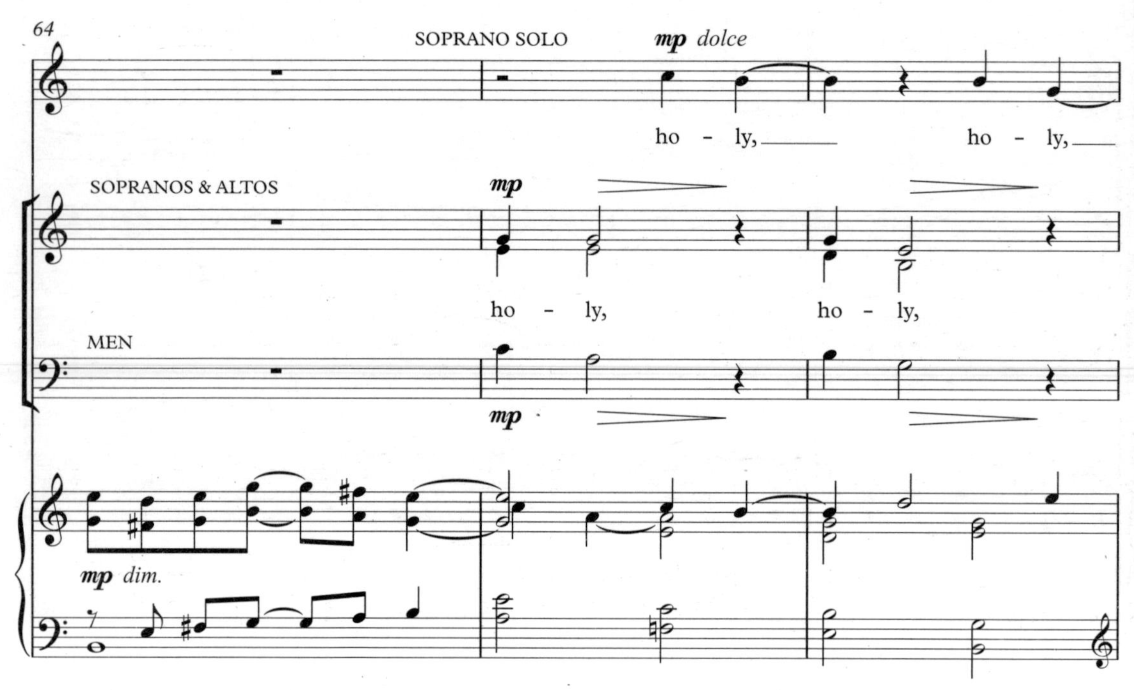
64
SOPRANO SOLO
mp dolce
ho - ly,
ho - ly,
SOPRANOS & ALTOS
mp
ho - ly,
ho - ly,
MEN
mp
mp dim.

67
p dim.
rall.
a tempo
ho - ly,
ho - ly,
p
ho - ly,
ho - ly,
ho - ly,
ho - ly,
p
ho - ly,
rall.
a tempo
p
mp espress.

71
SOPRANOS & ALTOS
UNISON
pp
mm
MEN
pp

75
p
pp
Ped.

Written for Christopher Connett and the choir of St Michael and All Angels, Mickleham

26. Trinity Sunday

Words: GEORGE HERBERT (1593-1633)
from THE TEMPLE (1633)

Music: STUART BEER

17
and san - ti - fied me to do good;
23
Sw. 8' Flute p
Sw. Strings pp
16' + Sw. pp
28
SOPRANOS
ALTOS
MEN
pp
Purge all my sins done here - to -
pp

34
fore: for I con - fess my hea - vy score, and I will strive to

41
pp
sin no more.
pp
Sw. 8' Flute p
Sw. Strings pp
16'+Sw. pp

47
SOPRANO
mp
En - rich my
ALTO
mp
En -
MEN
mp
mp
51
heart, mouth, hands in me, with faith, with
rich my heart, mouth, hands in me, with
mp
En - rich my heart, mouth, hands in me,

56
p
hope, with cha - ri - ty;
faith, with hope, with cha - ri -
with faith, with hope, with
61
mp
that I may run, rise, rest with
p
mp
ty; that I may run, rise,
p
mp
cha - ri - ty; that I may run, rise,

66
p
rit.
a tempo
thee.
p
rest with thee.
p
rest with thee.
rit.
a tempo
Sw. 8' Flute p
72
Sw. Strings pp
16' + Sw. pp
May 2016

For Fionn Lole on his fifth birthday

27. We meet you, O Christ

Words: Fred Kaan (1929–2009)

Music: Simon Lole

15
- ist in a shack. We see you the gard - 'ner, a tree on your
20
back.
ALTOS *mp*
Ah,
MEN *mf*
In
25
ah.
mil - lions a - live, a - way and a - broad, in - volved in our

SOPRANOS & ALTOS

poco cresc.

Im - pri-soned in sys-tems you

life you live down the road.

poco cresc.

long_ to be free._ We see you, Lord Je - sus, still bear - ing_ your

mp

A little slower

tree.__

p

We

mp

A little slower

mp

p

45
hear you, O Man, in a - go - ny cry. For free - dom you
50
mf
Your face in the pa - pers we
march, in ri - ots you die.
mf
55
f
read and we see. The tree must be plan - ted by hu - man de - cree.
f
f

Tempo I
61
SOPRANOS
ALTOS
f
You
MEN
f
You
Tempo I

65
f
You choose to be made at one with the earth; ah,
choose to be made at one with the earth; the dark of the
choose to be made at one with the earth; the dark of the

70
più f
Your death is your ris - ing, cre -
grave pre - pares for your birth. Your death is your ris - ing, cre -
75
ff
- a - tive your word: the tree springs to life, and our hope is re - stored.
- a - tive your word: the tree springs to life and our hope is re - stored.
81
poco rit.

Dorset, 2018

For Pauline

28. When Jesus Christ was yet a child

Words: Translated from the Russian by PERCY DEARMER

Music: GHISLAINE REECE-TRAPP

9
see - ing ro - ses on the tree, with shouts they plucked them mer - ri - ly.
see - ing ro - ses on the tree, with shouts they plucked them mer - ri - ly.
11
mp
3. 'Do you bind ro - ses
mp
3. 'Do you bind ro - ses
MEN mf
3. 'Do you bind ro - ses in your hair?', they
13
in your hair?' 'Take, take the
in your hair?' 'Take, take all but the
mp
cried in scorn to Je - sus there. The Boy said hum - bly: 'Take, I pray, all

15

na - ked thorns a - way, a- way, a -

na - ked thorns a - way, a- way, a -

but the na - ked thorns a - way, a - way, a -

Ped. 8' 16' *mp*

Più mosso, with determination

17

mf

way.' 4. Then of the thorns they made a crown, and

mf

way.' 4. Then of the thorns they made a crown, and

mf

way.' 4. Then of the thorns they made a crown, and

Più mosso, with determination

+ Oboe

mf *Sempre legato*

+ Oboe

mf

19
f
with rough fin - gers press'd it down, till on His fore - head fair and young, red
with rough fin - gers press'd it down, till on His fore - head fair and young, red
with rough fin - gers press'd it down, till on His fore - head fair and young, red
21
molto rit.
drops of blood like ro - ses sprung.
drops of blood like ro - ses sprung.
drops of blood like ro - ses sprung.
molto rit.
f
mf
mp

For Ben Lamb and the Choir of St Peter's Church, Bournemouth

29. When Mary came to the temple

(An anthem for Candlemas)

Words: DISRAELI BROWN
based on Luke 2

Music: DISRAELI BROWN

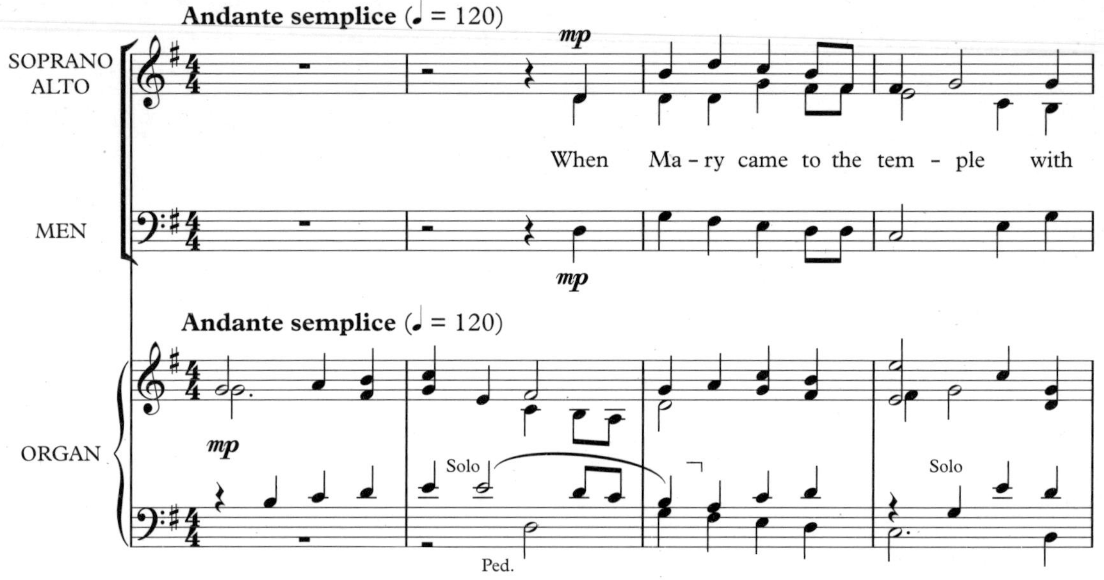

9

poco cresc.

word had been ful - filled; he took the in - fant in his arms, and

poco cresc.

poco cresc.

13

dim.

praised the Lord with a hum - ble voice:

* SOLO *senza rigor*

Lord, now let - test thou thy

dim.

Sw Strings

dim.

pp

(L.H.)

17

ser - vant de-part in peace, ac - cord - ing to thy word. For mine

* May be taken up the octave by a Soprano ad. lib.

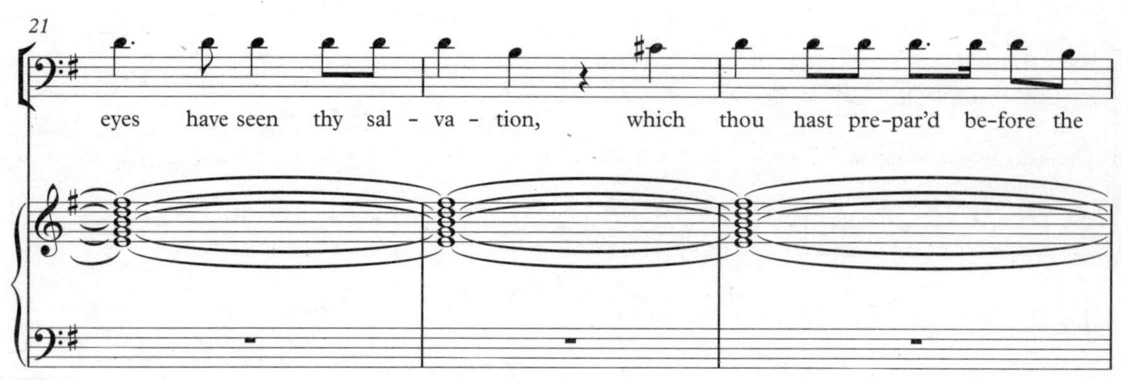
21
eyes have seen thy sal - va - tion, which thou hast pre-par'd be-fore the

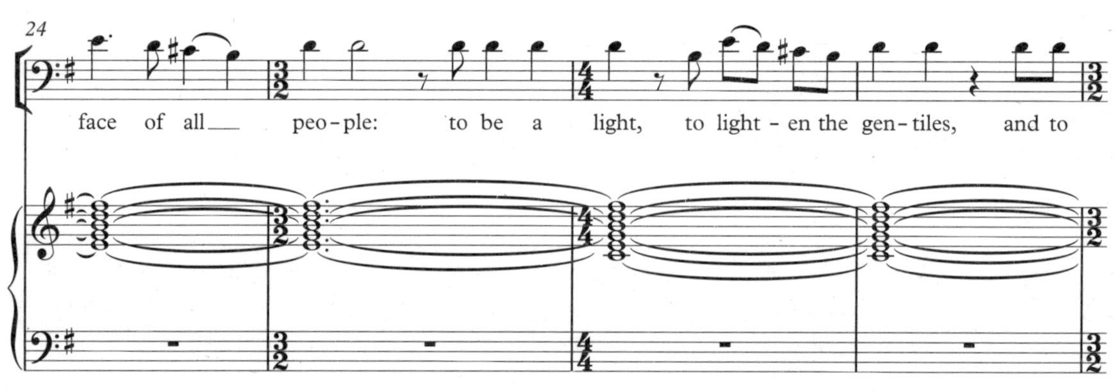
24
face of all peo-ple: to be a light, to light - en the gen-tiles, and to

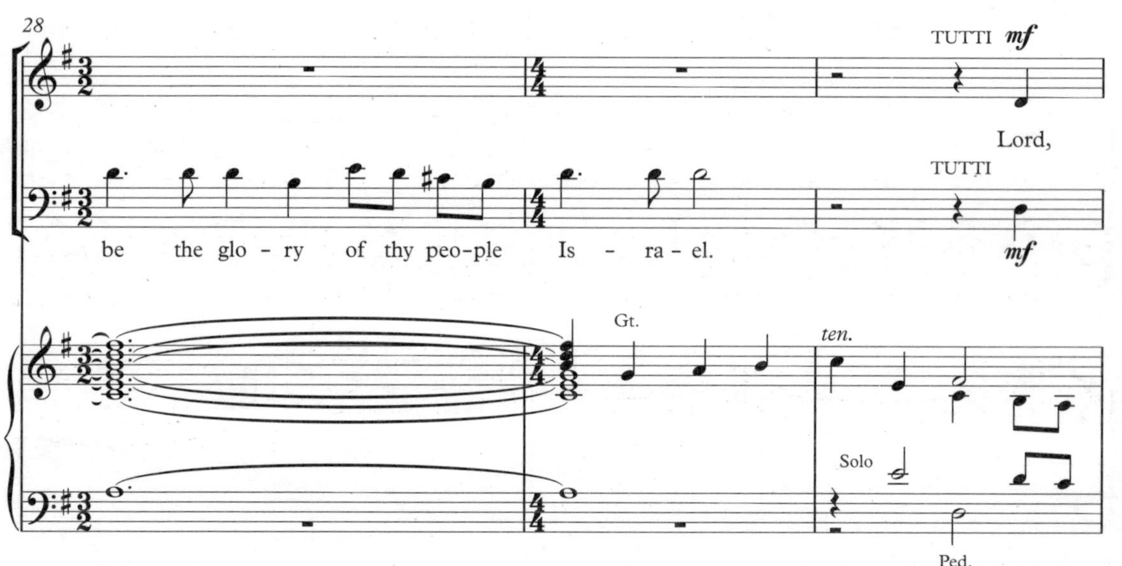
28
TUTTI *mf*
Lord,
TUTTI
be the glo - ry of thy peo-ple Is - ra - el.
mf
Gt.
ten.
Solo
Ped.

31
help us see our pur - pose as Si - meon saw your Son, and
mf
Solo
35
let us feel his con - tent - ment when our life's work is done, that
when
Solo
rit. e dim.
at the last, when we see you, our words may e - cho that
39
at the last, when we see you, our words may e - cho that
at the last, when we see you, our words may e - cho that
rit. e dim.

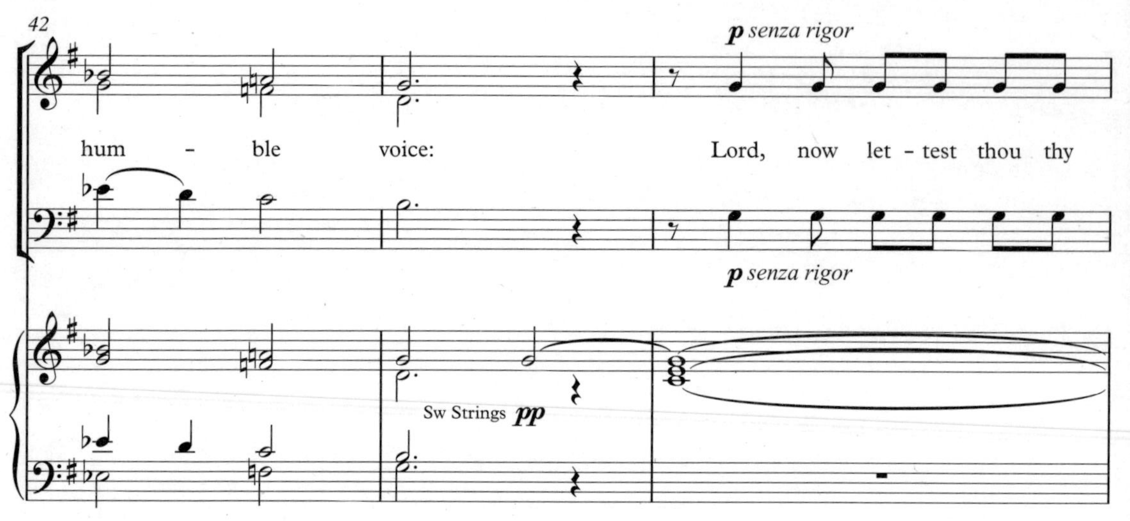

D.B. 23/1/04
Revised 17/6/18

30. The wounds of Christ

(an anthem for Saints' days)

Words: Austin Farrer (1904–1968)
from The Essential Sermons
adapted by the composer

Music: Sarah MacDonald

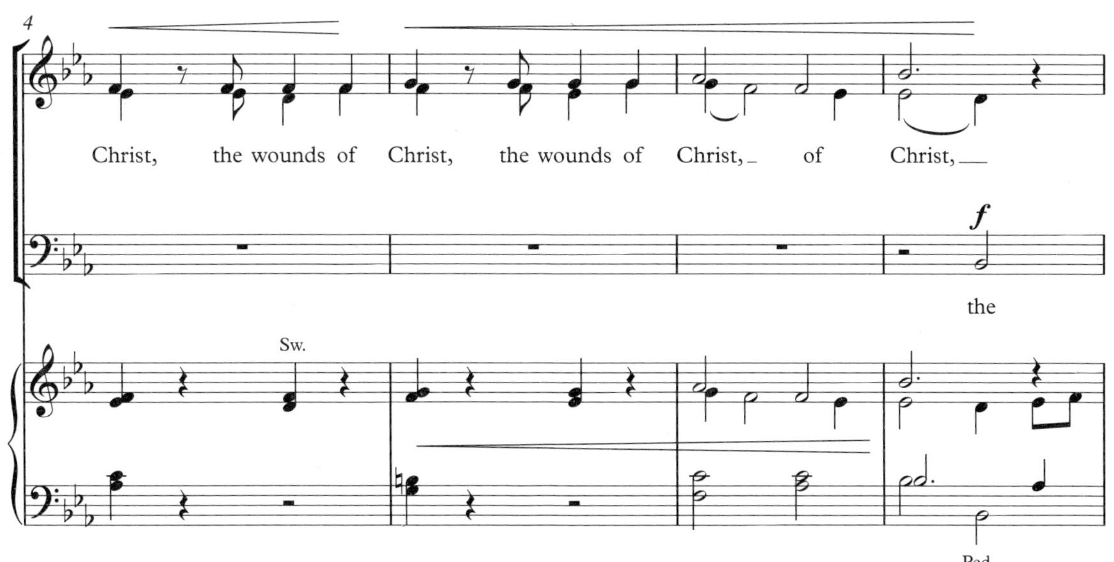

8
ALTOS
SOPRANOS & ALTOS
p
through which we touch the wounds of Christ; the
saints are the fin - gers through which we touch the wounds of Christ;
p
13
SOPRANOS
f
wounds of Christ; the saints are the fin - gers through which we touch the
f
18
ALTOS
p
SOPRANOS & ALTOS (unis.)
mf
wounds of Christ; the wounds of Christ; and the saints are the
p
the wounds of Christ;
p
mf
Man.
Ped.

23
eyes through which we meet his eyes;
and the ears through
27
p
hear his ut-ter-ance;
ALTOS mf
and u-
which we hear his ut-ter-ance;
mf
and u-
31
f
-ni - ting our-selves with them, u-ni - ting our-selves with
f
mf
f

36

SOPRANOS & ALTOS

f

them, — we re - ceive the o - ver - flow of their ho - li- ness, —

f

f

41

— the o - ver - flow of their ho - li- ness, —

46

mp

and we be - gin to know, we be - gin to know, we be - gin to know, — to

mf

Man.

50
ALTOS f
know,
that it is by God that we
f
that it is by God that we go to God,
f
Ped.

55
SOPRANO
div.
that we go to God, we
ALTO
go to God, we go to God, we
MEN
we go to God, we

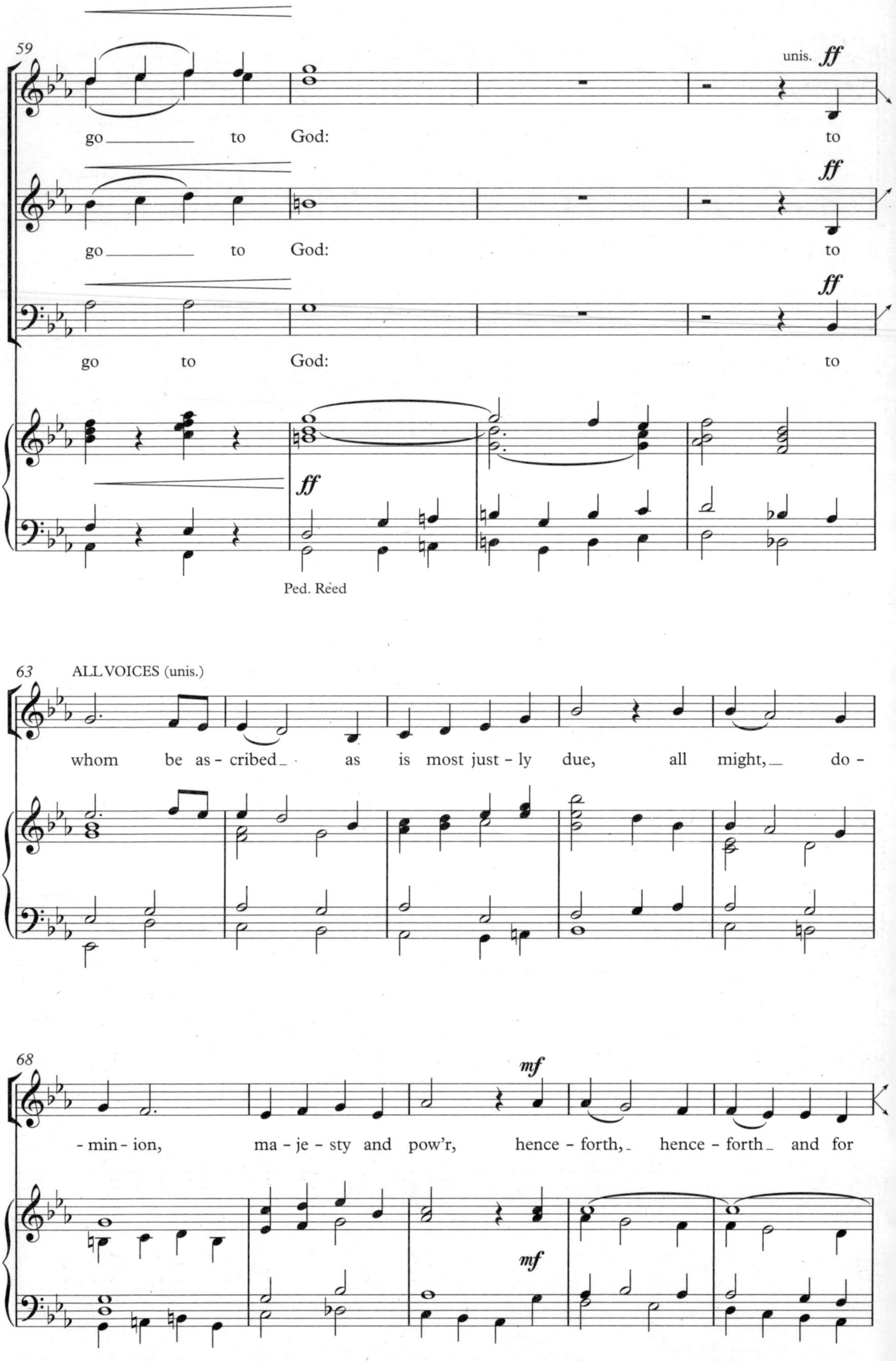

59

unis. *ff*

go to God: to

ff

go to God: to

ff

go to God: to

ff

Ped. Reed

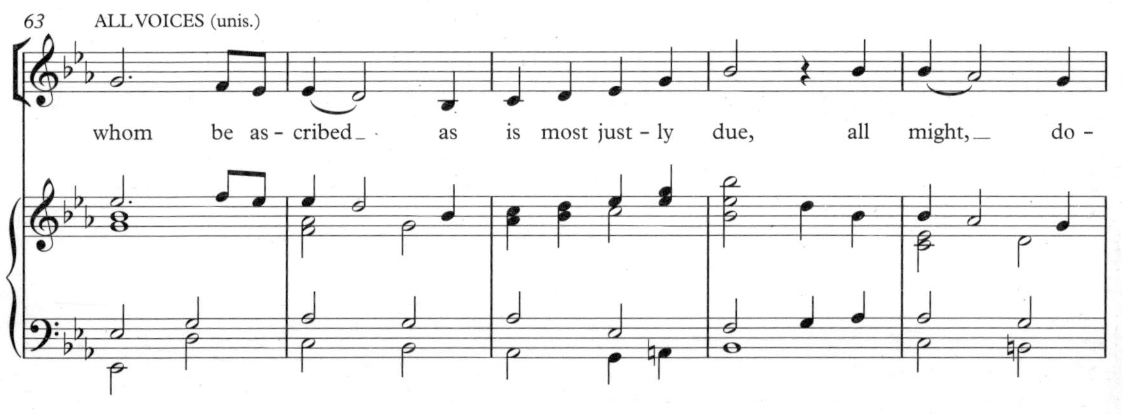

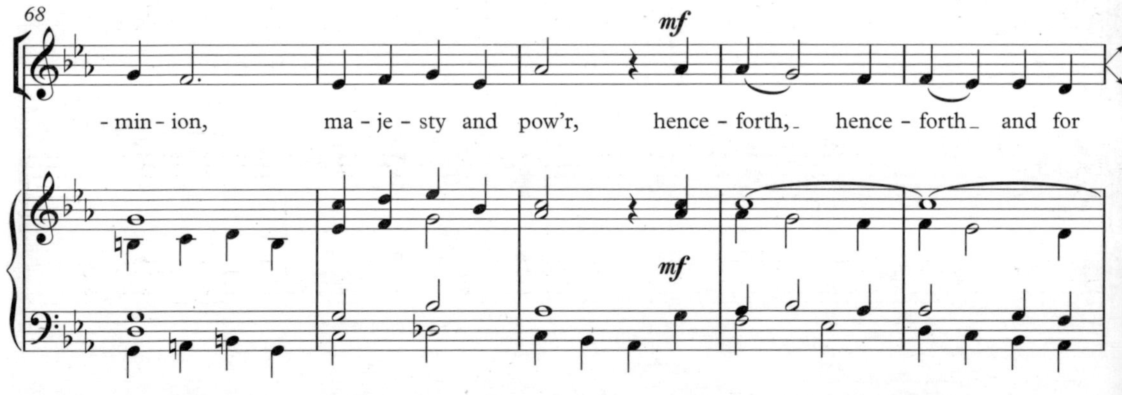

SOPRANOS & ALTOS
73
f
e - ver more. A - men, a - men, a - men,
MEN
f
f
78
f
a - men, a - men, a - men, al - le -
83
(optional Sop. solo)
ff
- lu - - ia! A - men.
ff
Solo Reed
Gt.
ff